MOTHER SH
WITCH AND PROF

Known for her reputedly amazingly accurate prophecies throughout the whole of the English-speaking world and beyond, this Tudor Yorkshirewoman – once rated more highly than Nostradamus – has been so wrapped around with fraud and fantasy that no serious historian has thought her worth a second glance . . . until now.

Enter Doctor Arnold Kellett who, in this book, presents the results of ten years' research tracing the evolution of a colourful character, renowned for her phenomenal ugliness, whose story involves such men as Cardinal Wolsey, Samuel Pepys, David Garrick and Charles Dickens, as well as a Restoration pornographer, a Victorian hoaxer and the purveyors of everything from soap to chapbooks forecasting Doomsday.

Illustrated with rare early woodcuts, prints and photographs, the book contains a lot of surprising discoveries. For instance, that Mother Shipton was without doubt the first Pantomime Dame, a kind of Fairy Godmother-in-Drag at Covent Garden in 1770s London, star of a long-running glittering extravaganza packed with spectacular transformation scenes; and that she was also widely celebrated in a Georgian popsong which ended every verse with the rousing refrain *'There's none like Mother Shipton!'* Indeed there is not.

A prestigious French museum currently displays a representation of her as 'the oldest known English puppet' and it has been discovered that a marionette in her likeness (which still exists) smoked a real pipe to popular acclaim on countrywide theatrical tours around Britain.

So did she *really* foresee the downfall of Cardinal Wolsey, the Gunpowder Plot, the Siege of York, the Great Fire of London, railway disasters, flying machines, the Internet and the End of the World? Arnold Kellett's investigation of all of these claims reads like a detective novel and shows us why this unique woman, even when disentangled from her legendary trappings, will survive far into the future she confidently attempted to probe.

By the same author:

The Knaresborough Story
Knaresborough in Old Picture Postcards
Historic Knaresborough
Basic Broad Yorkshire
'King John in Knaresborough'
    (*Yorkshire Archaeological Journal*)
Knaresborough: Archive Photographs
Kellett's Christmas
    (*a hundred poems*)
On Ilkla Mooar baht 'at: the Story of the Song
The Yorkshire Dictionary of Dialect, Tradition and Folklore

ARNOLD KELLETT

Mother Shipton
Witch and Prophetess

George Mann *of* Maidstone

MOTHER SHIPTON: WITCH AND PROPHETESS
by Arnold Kellett

Copyright © Arnold Kellett 2002

First published 2002
by George Mann

ISBN 0 7041 0402 4

Printed and bound in Great Britain
and published by
George Mann Books
PO Box 22, Maidstone
in the English County of Kent

Dedication

To our fifteen grandchildren,
with fervent hope for their unseen future.

.

Contents

Acknowledgements

Once again I am indebted to my wife, Pat, for valiant sessions of word-processing and putting up with a spreading clutter of books and papers. Thanks also to our daughter, Rachel, for help with proof-reading, and to Stan and Molly for help with the internet. I am also grateful to those who have provided or checked information, some many years ago, in particular Bernard Barr (York Minster Library), Michael Hine (Tourism Promotion Officer, Harrogate Borough Council), Jacqueline Simpson (The Folklore Society), John Adlard, J.A. Aldred, Dr. Frank Felsenstein, Paul Morgan, Malcolm Neesam, Adrian Sayers (Mother Shipton's Cave) and Aileen Osborn, for expert discussion of the Hereford Garrick Papers.

Librarians and archivists who have been especially helpful have been Dr. Beverley Hart and Catherine Haill (The Theatre Museum, London), Jon Cooter and Catherine Wilson (Hereford Museum), as well as assistants at the British Library (London and Boston Spa), the Victoria and Albert Museum, the Bodleian (Oxford), the Brotherton (The University of Leeds), and the reference libraries of York, Harrogate, Liverpool and Leeds.

Illustrations (including the cover) are mainly from my own collection. Permission to make use of others is gratefully acknowledged from the British Library (London), the Special Collections, the Brotherton Library (University of Leeds), the Musée de la Marionnette (Lyon), Peter Kearney, the North Yorkshire County Library, Vic Lokie (postcards) and Frank Newbould (photograph of cave).

Author's Preface

The name of Mother Shipton is known throughout the English-speaking world. It is the first and probably the only name that will spring to mind if we are asked to think of an English witch. The prophecies attributed to her, once as famous as those of her French contemporary, Nostradamus, have constantly been reprinted – with embellishments – ever since the mid-seventeenth century.

Yet she remains a figure of mystery, obscured and distorted by muddled mythology more than any other female in English folklore. Who *was* Mother Shipton? Did she exist as a historical person? And, if so, when and where? What are her prophecies? Are they genuine, in the sense that she uttered them? Or were they put into her mouth by writers of pamphlets and chapbooks? Are any of her prophecies genuine in the sense that they were actually fulfilled? Or were they all printed after the events had taken place? (An infallible method of getting them right!)

Such questions are answered in the following pages, which I hope will read rather like a piece of detective-work. This, for me, has always been the appeal of historical and literary research. It involves tracking down clues and witnesses, sifting the evidence – in this case disentangling the real Mother Shipton from the fanciful trappings woven round her by centuries of spin-doctors. Yet it is the evolution of her image that I find so interesting. Who would have suspected her role as a pipe-smoking puppet – or the first pantomime dame – or the woman with a profile so distinctively hideous that it is stamped on the wings of a common British moth?

Fascination with Mother Shipton was aroused by my first childhood visit to Knaresborough. Here, in this picturesque North Yorkshire town she is alive and thriving. Visitors come from all over the world to see the ruined Castle in its spectacular setting above the fairy-tale gorge of the Nidd. They look down on the lovely riverside woodland through which the Long Walk leads to the magical petrifactions of the Dropping Well, the Wishing Well and Mother Shipton's Cave. They hear of the many remarkable characters associated with Knaresborough – Hugh de Morville and the murderers of Becket, King John, Saint Robert, Piers Gaveston, Queen Philippa, Guy Fawkes, Blind Jack and the rest . . . But most of all they come because of Mother Shipton.

Since 1956 I have put down deep roots in this unique town, researching every aspect of the history of Knaresborough and, in particular, being awarded the Bramley History Prize for work on Mother Shipton, and more recently being invited to write an 'official' account of her for the *New National Dictionary of Biography*.

Here, then, is the gist of what I have discovered, over ten years of research, about this curious lady and her bizarre prophecies. I did not set out to discredit and debunk – though exposure of fraud and foolishness is an inevitable consequence of the enquiry. It is rather that I have tried to say, with an early television detective, (Sergeant Friday in 'Dragnet') 'Just give me the facts, ma'am!' As a local historian I feel it is high time we made a serious investigation into the case of this obscure local woman who has reached international fame, yet who, because she has been packaged in so much fanciful nonsense, has never been taken seriously by historians.

I hope you will find this a book you can read through from the beginning, rather than one to be dipped into, and that as you read on, you will agree that truth really is stranger – and more entertaining – than fiction. Demythologising can be fun – and can do no harm to Mother Shipton. She will surely survive as a colourful figure and talking-point far into the future she attempted to probe.

Arnold Kellett,
Knaresborough, North Yorkshire, 2002

SCOTLAND

Melrose •

WALES

Knaresborough •
• YORK
• Cawood •

Kinver Edge •

Downham Market •
Yarmc

• Buckingham
•
Rollright Stones

LONDON •

Porlock •
• Williton
• Yeovil
Portsmouth Brighton

*A Map showing locations which
have traditional associations with
Mother Shipton*

xi

1

Enter Mother Shipton: the Death of Wolsey

Mother Shipton has an air of mystery about her from the beginning. She suddenly appears on the scene in the days of Charles I, though she was, in fact, a Tudor prophetess, said to have been born around 1488. Whatever the strength of the oral tradition that had preceded it, the earliest-known published reference to her is in an anonymous pamphlet printed in 1641. It is entitled *The Prophesie of Mother Shipton in the Raigne of King Henry the Eighth*, printed in London by Richard Lownds, 'at his shop adjoyning to Ludgate'. It is extremely scarce, with only two or three copies surviving. The one in the British Library was presented by George III.

This 1641 Pamphlet tells us nothing about the date or place of Mother Shipton's birth, but opens abruptly with an account of her prophecy concerning the proposed visit of Cardinal Wolsey to York, and his angry threat to have her burnt as a witch for saying he would never reach the city. There is no indication of how this and her other prophecies were conceived. As there is no mention here of astrology the impression is that she was a clairvoyante, a woman who glimpsed the future through second sight.

There is firm historical evidence to show that Wolsey intended his enthronement in York Minster to take place on the 7th November 1530, and from the context in the pamphlet we can conclude that Mother Shipton was living in York itself shortly before this time. The fulfilment of her prediction about Wolsey presumably brought her to national fame, which is why the writer of the pamphlet, even as late as 1641, apparently saw no need to give any kind of biographical introduction. Everybody in seventeenth-century England, it seems, had heard of Mother Shipton.

It is significant that somebody decided to put her into print in 1641. This was a year buzzing with rumour and propaganda in a turbulent England on the eve of the Civil War. Both Royalists and Parliamentarians had a lively interest in prophecy, each side hoping to use it as propaganda, especially millenarian forecasts of national disasters. Mother Shipton was just one voice amongst many, but –

apart from even vaguer figures like Merlin – one of the earliest. Moreover, she was a woman, and this was a time when early feminists saw prophesying as the only way, as Keith Thomas observed, in which they 'could hope to disseminate their opinions on public events'.

It would be very satisfying to find documentary or printed evidence to establish beyond any doubt that Mother Shipton really existed as a historical person. Yet, over the past thirty years I have searched in vain for any reference earlier that 1641 – and even this is only in the pamphlet referred to, which was printed well over a century after the events it describes. This embarrassingly large gap no doubt explains why one version of the pamphlet, also printed in London in 1641, claims that it is 'A True Coppie of Mother Shipton's Last Prophecies: As they were taken from one Joane Waller in the year of our Lord 1625, Who died in March last 1641, being ninety-four yeares of age'. This would mean that the girl was not born until 1547, already seventeen years after the Wolsey prediction, and she must have been about 78 before she recorded her memories of Mother Shipton. But at least this claim to have an oral witness strengthens the probability that the prophetess was a real woman and not someone invented.

A reference by Henry VIII to 'the Witch of York' at first sight looks like early evidence, but from the context – a letter to the Duke of Norfolk, who was engaged in rounding up the King's enemies in 1537 – it almost certainly refers to Mabel Brigge, a York woman who was executed as a witch the following year. The principal evidence concerned Mabel's refusal to drink milk in an attempt to force the King and the Duke to return her property.

This was interpreted as 'fasting a Black Fast to an abominable intent' – and it confirms that Wolsey's threat to have Mother Shipton burnt was typical of the time.

No doubt he assumed that she had performed a 'Black Fast' against him. Once a hostile prophecy had been made it was presumed that the prophet intended to bring about some calamity by means of witchcraft.

My hopes of finding an early and even a contemporary reference to Mother Shipton were raised in the 1960s when I read of the discovery of a mention of her in a document believed to be 'late fifteenth or early sixteenth century'.

This claim appeared in a new edition of *Mother Shipton's Prophecies* published in Knaresborough, which asserted that a passage referring to her had been found in the *'Liber Elemosinatoris'* in the archives of Durham University.

Alia Prenosticacio Ursule Sondyal?
When hongry men schall wryte and hear
The saiying(s) of the covelyng seere
Then all the woorld schal come to view
The auncient toun of Knar(is)boroo

This seemed far too good to be true – and quite uncharacteristic of the period it was supposed to be from, including the patently bogus spelling of Knaresborough in a form found nowhere else. The title, intended to be translated as 'Other prophecies of Ursule Sondyal', looks like a reference to Ursula Sonthiel – one of the later versions of Mother Shipton's maiden name. But its closeness to 'Ursula Sundial' shows it to be a satirical comment on the supposed name of the prophetess.

My suspicions were confirmed when I looked into the alleged source of this quotation . . . The document, correctly spelt the *Liber Elemosinaris*, does indeed exist among the Muniments of the Dean and Chapter of Durham. But the part from which the Shipton quote was supposed to be taken (folio 35 r) dates from the early thirteenth century and refers entirely to legal matters concerning the county of Durham.

Where, then, had this Mother Shipton passage come from?

The writer of the booklet could hardly have made it up, since the Acknowledgements stated that it had been obtained from Durham University. When I contacted the university I was eventually told that in about 1965 a member of the staff had visited Mother Shipton's Cave in Knaresborough. On his return to Durham he had sent a letter claiming to have discovered this passage about 'Ursula Sondyal'.

The spoof information, sent as a kind of experiment, was accepted and published in good faith – a hoax illustrating just how cautious we must be in sifting through the Mother Shipton material. This is by no means the first – or the last – piece of fakery to be foisted on this long-suffering Yorkshirewoman.

In the absence of anything earlier let us examine the 1641

Pamphlet. This opens with Mother Shipton's dramatic prediction that Cardinal Wolsey, appointed Archbishop of York by Henry VIII, would never even reach the city whose name formed part of his title:

When shee heard King Henry the eighth should be King, and Cardinal Wolsey should be at Yorke, shee said that Cardinall Wolsey should never come to Yorke with the King, and the Cardinall hearing, being angry, sent the Duke of Suffolke, the Lord Piercy, and the Lord Darcy to her, who came with their men disguised to the King's house neere Yorke, where leaving their men, they went to Master Besley to Yorke, and desired him to goe with them to Mother Shipton's house, where when they came they knocked at the doore, shee said Come in Master Besley, and those honourable Lords with you, and Master Besley would have put in the Lords before him, but shee said, come in Master Besley, you know the way, but they doe not. This they thought strange, that shee should know them, and never saw them.

To understand the significance of this passage it is necessary to remind ourselves of certain well-established facts about Cardinal Wolsey. A remarkably ambitious and able man, Thomas Wolsey, son of an Ipswich inn-keeper and butcher, was educated at Oxford, ordained a priest in 1498, and appointed chaplain to Henry VII in 1507.

When Henry VIII became king two years later he first appointed Wolsey as privy counsellor, then Bishop of Lincoln, and soon afterwards Archbishop of York. Wolsey officially held this appointment from the 1st October, 1514, the date of a Bull issued by Pope Leo X, but he showed no inclination to visit York, and was installed as archbishop by proxy.

One reason for his failure to travel north was his deep involvement in state affairs in London, for the following year he was appointed Lord Chancellor of England and then made Cardinal by the Pope. In this position Wolsey wielded immense power, and soon became hated because of his domineering manner, bad temper and extravagance. Even though he never visited York once in the sixteen years he was archbishop, he used his authority to have silver coins minted in the city.

In evidence against him it was stated to Henry VIII that 'the said Lord Cardinal, of his further pompous and presumptuous mind, hath enterprized to imprint the Cardinal's hat under your arms on your coin of groats made at your city of York, which like deed hath not been seen or done by any subject before within your realme'.

Mother Shipton's utterance no doubt reflected the distaste the people of York felt for Wolsey, and a shrewd observer might conclude that the archbishop was so preoccupied with the King's affairs that he would have neither the time nor the interest even to visit York. Resentment over Wolsey's insulting lack of interest in the city was still felt in Victorian times.

'It is a remarkable circumstance', wrote a commentator in 1847, 'that the distinguished prelate, Thomas Wolsey, who held the See of York at a time when the rebuilding of the Cathedral Church of his diocese, after a course of nearly three centuries, was completed, never saw the magnificent structure, or only saw it at a distance. Nor is it probable that he would ever have thought of visiting it, had he not fallen into disgrace at the court'.

It is entirely credible that a man of Wolsey's temperament and style, having heard through one of his spies and informers that a woman in York was speaking disparagingly of him, would send somebody to investigate and then silence her.

Typical of the Tudor age, Wolsey took prediction very seriously. According to his biographer and close associate, George Cavendish, on one occasion Wolsey had expressed his concern about the rhymed prophecy:

> When the Cowe ridyth the Bull,
> Then, Priest, beware thy Scull!

This was sometimes attributed to Mother Shipton, and usually interpreted as referring to the 'Cowe' (Henry VIII) marrying the 'Bull' (Anne Boleyn, whose crest was the head of a black bull). An anonymous contemporary verse about the Cardinal's superstitious recourse to prognosticators shows how insecure he must have felt:

> He counseled (men saide) with Astronomyers
> (Or what other secte I cannot well saye,
> Weare they Sothesayers or weare they lyers)
> Whether he shoulde fall or florysche alwaye;
> Whose answeare was, he should come to decaye
> By meanys (they founde) of a certayne woman.

This 'certayne woman' might well bring Mother Shipton to mind, but this refers either to Catherine of Aragon, the first wife of Henry VIII, whose divorce from the king Wolsey failed to obtain, or alternatively to Anne Boleyn, Catherine's lady-in-waiting. As the prospective second queen, she naturally encouraged Henry's impatience with Wolsey, becoming the principal instigator of his fall from grace.

For complex political reasons the Cardinal was unable to obtain a Papal dispensation to annul the marriage to Catherine, and so, in 1529, he was tried and found guilty of praemunire for illegally holding office from the Pope. Wolsey was dismissed from his post as Lord Chancellor and deprived of all his property, but he was allowed to remain Archbishop of York, which explains why, at long last, he travelled north to his episcopal residence of Cawood Castle, about eight miles south of York.

In spite of his diminished status Wolsey recovered sufficiently to maintain an expensive household and a display of pomp. He left Southwell for Cawood, with no fewer than six hundred horsemen in his train. Once he had settled in, he fixed his unconscionably delayed enthronement as Archbishop of York for the 7th November, 1530, and there is every indication that he intended to make it a most impressive demonstration of the fact that he still held high office. It is true that Cavendish denied this, claiming that Wolsey was really quite a humble man, and given the warmest possible welcome by the Yorkshire people, who told him that during his long absence they had been 'all that while like fatherlesse childerne and comfortlesse, trusting shortly to see hyme among them in his owen chirche'.

They had even wanted, according to Cavendish, to provide a carpet for their archbishop to walk on all the way from outside the gates of York to the Minster, but he had refused, saying 'I take God to be my very juge that I presume not to go thether for any tryumphe or vaynglory'. Another source, however, says that Wolsey issued an order to 'all the lordes, abbottes, priors, knights, esquiers and gentlemen' of the diocese to be at Cawood on the eve of his enthronement so they could 'bring him to York with all manner of pompe and solemnitie'.

Given these circumstances, to allow Mother Shipton to persist with her prediction that he would never even reach the city was something Wolsey could not tolerate. We can therefore assume that it was during this preparatory period that he, 'being angry', sent the three lords to seek out the troublesome prophetess. All three were officers, but they went in disguise, presumably as ordinary gentlemen, so as not to draw public attention to the archbishop's concern. They first left their soldiers at 'the King's house', that is, the present King's Manor, just outside the city walls, where Henry VIII himself stayed in 1541.

The three 'honourable Lords' were the kind of men we might have expected Wolsey to use as his secret inquisitors. The Duke of Suffolk was Henry Grey, who succeeded to the title of the Third Marquis of Dorset in 1530 and married Frances, daughter of the Duke of Suffolk. Henry was the father of Lady Jane Grey, who, some twenty-three years later was to reign as a tragic Queen of nine days. The Duke had been Marshall of the Royal Household since 1511, and owed much to Wolsey – yet was instrumental in his fall from favour.

'The Lord Piercy' was Thomas Percy, member of the famous Northumberland family. He was brother and heir presumptive to Henry Algernon Percy, the Sixth Earl of Northumberland, who had served as a page and servant in Wolsey's household and, incidentally, had a clandestine love-affair with Anne Boleyn. At that time the Lord Percy who visited Mother Shipton was Lord of Spofforth, near Knaresborough, from where he could easily have travelled to York.

A similarly short journey could have been made by the third Lord, Thomas D'Arcy, who was then Steward of the Honour of Knaresborough, presumably resident in Knaresborough Castle. He was, in fact, one of the peers who supported the King in his petition to divorce Catherine, and had signed the bill of articles against Wolsey in 1529. So, like the Duke, his loyalty might have been divided and he had come to see Mother Shipton more out of curiosity than indignation on Wolsey's behalf.

Who was this 'Master Besley' whom they pressed into service as a guide? When I put this question to Bernard Barr of the York Minster Library he recalled having transcribed details about a York lawyer by the name of Reynold or Reginald Besely from records in St. Mary's Tower, York. He agreed that the period and circumstances certainly justified an identification of 'Master Besley' as this local lawyer. Reynold Besely had a successful practice, and in 1542 was appointed Clerk to the Council and County Court. In 1553 he was elected as one of Knaresborough's first two MPs, and in the following year he became Notary and Advocate to the Court of York, and was made a Freeman of the city. The three lords probably called for him at his home in Coney Street, a substantial house with a garth on the banks of the River Ouse – but he had another large house, just outside Micklegate Bar.

There is something historically convincing about the references to Besely in the 1641 Pamphlet. His services would be invaluable. As a legal man he would be suitable to act as an intermediary, all the more so because he clearly knew Mother Shipton well. He also knew the way to her house. This was stated in a later pamphlet to have been at 'Ring-house' or even 'Drying-houses'. This could have been the part of York known as Dringhouses, but is more likely to have been a careless transposition of the original 'King's House', where the lords first called.

The account continues with a reference to Mother Shipton's hospitality round a blazing fire. This would be consistent with the onset of winter – late October or early November, just before Wolsey's intended enthronement:

and then they went into the house, where there was a great fire, and shee bade them welcome, calling them all by their names, and sent for some Cakes and Ale, and they drunke and were very merry. Mother Shipton, said the Duke, if you knew what wee come about, you would not make us so welcome, and shee said the messenger should not be hang'd; Mother Shipton, said the Duke, you said the Cardinall should never see Yorke; Yea, said shee, I said hee might see Yorke, but never come at it; But said the Duke, when he comes to Yorke thou shalt be burned; Wee shall see that, said shee, and plucking her Handker-chieffe off her head shee threw it into the fire, and it would not burne, then she tooke her staffe and turned it into the fire, and it would not burne, then she tooke it and put it on again; Now (said the Duke) what meane you by this? If this had burn'd (said shee) I might have burned.

It is interesting to see that whereas Mother Shipton refers to a proverb about hanging, the punishment she is threatened with is burning. The burning of witches (rather than hanging) was unusual in England, a rare example being at Pocklington, just to the east of York, where in 1630 'old wife Greene' was burnt in the market place 'for a witch'. But burning was a standard punishment for heretical utterances, and as Mother Shipton was deemed to have spoken ill of the Archbishop himself, Wolsey could easily have arranged for her to be burnt at the stake.

One of the first displays of witches' magic attributed to Mother Shipton is this spectacular trick of taking her kerchief and stick – the ones no doubt shown in early portraits – unscathed from a great fire. If it occurred as described it was a convincing demonstration to Wolsey's men that 'the lady's not for burning'. The theme of immunity from flames is an ancient one, an early example being found in the Old Testament in the story of the three men cast into Nebuchadnezzar's burning fiery furnace, where we read that the fire had no power over them, 'nor was an hair of their head singed, neither were their coats changed'.

It is also a theme we find in folklore, such as in stories of burnt clothing restored by magic. Whatever lies behind this report of Mother Shipton's demonstration, allegedly recorded by eye-witnesses, it is easy to show how later writers have embroidered on it. For example, we can compare the following version from a 1686 account with the passage quoted above, noting that a significant length of time is now given (to obviate any suggestion that the kerchief was rapidly popped in and out of the flames) and that the material was completely unmarked, as though made fireproof:

Then taking off her Linen Kerchief from her head, saies she, If this burn, then I may burn, and immediately flung it into the fire before them, but it would not burn, so that after it had lain in the flames a quarter of an hour, she took it out again not so much as singed.

The writer of the 1641 Pamphlet implies that the three noble lords were most impressed by Mother Shipton's occult powers. Immediately they had witnessed the incombustibility of her kerchief and staff, they forgot about Wolsey's fate and began to ask her about their own – rather in the manner of people cadging a diagnosis from a doctor they have met socially:

Mother Shipton (quoth the Duke) what thinke you of me? My love, said shee, the time will come when you will be as low as I am, and that's a low one indeed. My Lord Percy said, what say you of me? My Lord (said shee) shoe your Horse in the quicke, and you shall doe well, but your body will bee buried in Yorke pavement, and your head shall be stolne from the barre and carried into France. Then said

Lord Darcy, and what thinke you of me? Shee said, you have made a great Gun, shoot it off, for it will doe you no good, you are going to warre, you will paine many a man, but you will kill none, so they went away.

Several interesting points arise from this passage. At first sight Mother Shipton's use of 'my love' when addressing a personage like the Duke of Suffolk – whose identity we are told she knew, in spite of his disguise – sounds like the authentic speech of an elderly Yorkshirewoman, whose successors, speaking contemporary Yorkshire dialect, still use the friendly *luv*. Later editions assume that this apparent over-familiarity might have been a misprint, and change it to 'my lord'.

Were these predictions about the three lords fulfilled? There is no historical doubt that each of them came to a tragic end . . . The Duke of Suffolk, Henry Grey, joined the rebellion led by Sir Thomas Wyatt against Queen Mary. For this he was arrested for high treason at Westminster Hall, found guilty and beheaded on Tower Hill on the 23rd February 1554. Both Lord Percy and Lord Darcy took part in the Pilgrimage of Grace of 1536, the uprising of northern Catholics in protest over the radical changes being made by Henry VIII. The following year Henry retaliated with characteristic ferocity, ordering the execution of about 200 rebels, including Lord Percy and Lord Darcy. The former was beheaded on the 2nd June, the latter on Tower Hill on the 30th June, 1537.

As this 1641 edition of Mother Shipton was published more than a century after the deaths of these men, it could be dismissed as something constructed on events which had already taken place, and therefore worthless as a record of prophecy. On the other hand, if the writer had simply been putting into the mouth of Mother Shipton certain historical facts, we would have expected him to have more details.

He might, for example, have predicted Lord Darcy's execution, rather than have made the vague forecast that his military activities would come to nothing.

The famous Civil War astrologer William Lilly certainly believed that Mother Shipton had predicted these deaths, and in his own edition of the prophecies (1645) he adds this marginal note opposite the Percy reference: 'This proved true, for he rose in rebellion in the north; and by not fleeing when he might, was taken and beheaded in Yorke, where his body was buried, and his head was stolen and carried into France'.

Confirmation of some of this is provided by Drake, the eighteenth-century York historian. He tells us that Percy was beheaded on a specially-erected scaffold on the Pavement. Two of his servants buried his body in the churchyard of St. Crux, but his head was displayed on the tall pole in Micklegate Bar, where it remained for two years 'but was afterwards stolen from thence'.

The important passage which follows the reported consultation of the three lords about their fortunes is presented as an indisputable confirmation of Mother Shipton's prediction that Wolsey would see York, but never reach the city:

Not long after the Cardinall came to Cawood, and going to the top of the Tower, hee asked where Yorke was, and how farre it was thither, and said that one had said hee should never see Yorke; Nay, said one, shee said you might see Yorke, but never come at it. He vowed to burne her when he came to Yorke. Then they shewed him Yorke, and told him it was but eight miles thence; he said he will soone be there; but being sent for by the King hee dyed in the way to London at Lecester of a laske; and Shipton's wife said to Master Besley, yonder is a fine stall built for the Cardinall in the Minster, of Gold, Pearle, and precious stone, goe and present one of the pillers to King Henry, and hee did so.

This was the prophecy by which Mother Shipton was best known, and appeared in some form in most of the later pamphlets and chapbooks, some with a woodcut showing Wolsey gazing towards York from the tower of Cawood Castle, confronted by a baleful Mother Shipton of truly witch-like appearance, with Henry VIII looking on. Variants of the story appeared, but were insignificant. A 1686 pamphlet, for example, says that Wolsey was anxious to reach York:

For (quoth he) there was a Witch said, I should never see York. Nay, says one present, your Eminence is misinformed, she said you should see it, but not come at it. Then he vow'd to burn her when he came there . . but behold, immediately he was sent for back by the King, and dyed of a violent looseness at Leicester.

The little dramatic touch provided by the addition of 'behold,

23

immediately . . .' makes the point that no sooner had Wolsey uttered this threat against Mother Shipton than he was 'sent for' by Henry VIII. In later versions the dramatic timing is stressed even more. In a 1743 account we read that having vowed from the tower-top to burn the witch:

e'er he descended the Stairs a Message arriv'd from the King to demand his presence forthwith; so he was obliged to return directly, and being took with a violent looseness at Leicester he gave up the Ghost in his Journey, which verify'd the Prophecy in every Degree.

What are the facts about Wolsey's recall to London? In the first place they are more dramatic than these pamphlets suggest. He was not requested to return by the King, but arrested at Cawood on a charge of high treason.

Cavendish, who was an eye-witness of this, tells us of an ominous sign which occurred during dinner, shortly before the arrest, when a heavy silver cross fell and caught the head of a member of Wolsey's entourage, drawing blood.

Cavendish does not describe the conversation with Wolsey on top of the tower, but he was absent for a time in York, arranging details of the enthronement, and his silence here is no proof that his story was invented.

What he does tell us is that on the 4th November, only three days before the proposed enthronement, Lord Northumberland had unexpectedly arrived at Cawood with a party of soldiers. The Cardinal wined and dined him, and all was cordial until Northumberland went with Wolsey to the latter's bedroom then, in the words of Cavendish:

tremlying sayed with a very faynt and softe voyce unto my lord, layeing his hand upon his arme My lord, quoth he, I arrest you of hyghe treason, with which wordes my lord was marvelously astonyed, standyng both still a long space without any ferther wordes . . .

Cavendish adds that the next day Wolsey looked so upset that 'it wold have caused the flyntiest hart to have relented and burst for sorrowe . . . there was not a drie eye among all the gentilmen sytting at the table with him'.

Mother Shipton confronting Cardinal Wolsey,
who is seen looking toward York from Cawood Castle
(1642 Pamphlet, title-page. British Library)

The arresting-party did not have a change of heart, however, and set off with their prisoner for London, the people of Yorkshire, according to Cavendish, shouting out as Wolsey was conducted through the streets how much they loved him.

Records show that the sum of forty pounds was paid for 'the conveyance of the cardinal of York to the Tower', but he never arrived. On the way south, he became ill with dysentery and fever, and was taken to Leicester Abbey, where he died on the 29th November, 1530, almost his last words being the much-quoted 'If I had served my God with half the zeal that I have served my King, he would not, in my grey hairs, have thus forsaken me'. It is to be hoped that Wolsey's shameful neglect of York was included in these final repentant thoughts.

There is no doubt that Wolsey's meteoric downfall and death was a great sensation, especially in Yorkshire. The effect was admirably described by Drake, writing in 1736 in his *Eboracum*: 'We see our prelate now like a meteor, at his height and the fullness of his lustre; which he no sooner arrived at, but he more suddenly fell'. It was Drake, however, who was the first to cast doubt on the validity of Mother Shipton's prophecy about Wolsey. He wrote:

This prelate never was at York, though he came so near it as Cawood; which makes good a prophecy of Mother Shipton, esteemed an old witch in those days, who foretold, he should see York, but never come at it. I should not have mentioned this idle story, but that it is fresh in the mouths of our country people at this day; but whether it was a real prediction, or raised after the event, I shall not take upon me to determine. It is more than probable, like all the rest of these kind of tales, the accident gave occasion to the story.

Sceptical though Drake is, his testimony that the story was still being circulated by country folk some two hundred years after 1530 argues in favour of a strong oral tradition. Such people would mostly be illiterate and unlikely to be influenced by the seventeeth-century pamphlets. They could, of course, simply have been maintaining no more than something generated by the gossip that must surely have followed Wolsey's death.

One thing is obvious. If the 1641 account of the prophecy had been entirely fabricated by someone wise after the event, he could scarcely have resisted the temptation to arrange for Mother Shipton not only to have predicted the execution of Lord Darcy, but also to have prophesied Wolsey's arrest for high treason and his ensuing death at Leicester, especially when this came about through a violent bowel infection striking him down like an act of malevolent witchcraft. As it is, no reason whatever was given to explain why the Cardinal would not reach York.

It is this very lack of detail, this very haziness and reticence, which makes the 1641 Pamphlet a reasonable piece of evidence that there may have existed in Tudor York a wise-woman who told fortunes, and suddenly attained national celebrity through her comments about a controversial public figure. Whether these arose out of genuine clairvoyance or shrewd observation, the best explanation of how she became known far beyond the bounds of her native Yorkshire is that she had either glimpsed or guessed that something bad was going to happen to Wolsey – and had not hesitated to declare it.

Even writers sceptical about the Shipton prophecies conceded that she had become a legend in her lifetime. In 1642, as though to comment on the pamphlet published the year before, another appeared in Latin, the *Nuncius Propheticus*, referring to this woman who had lived 'more than a hundred years ago'. Yet, says the writer, he feels sure she really lived and prophesied, because ordinary people are still singing about her and reciting her words as though she were the divinely enlightened '*Sibylla Eboracensis*', the Sibyl of York.

Mother Shipton
from
The Strange and Wonderful History of Mother Shipton (1686)

2

Prophecies of Doom and Disaster

After the downfall and death of Wolsey, so impressed was Master Besely that, according to the 1641 Lownds Pamphlet, 'seeing these things fall out as shee had foretold', he paid another visit to Mother Shipton, and requested her to give him more of her prophecies. As we have noted, Reynold Besely was a well-educated man, an advocate involved in civic and ecclesiastical affairs, and it is not unreasonable to suppose that the series of prophecies which constitute the remainder of the pamphlet are based on notes which he originally made in the presence of Mother Shipton. Alternatively, we may suppose that they came from an oral tradition linked with his name – but, in either case, there is no doubt that the content indicates a source firmly rooted in York.

Mother Shipton was apparently only too willing to oblige Master Besely, and she launched forth into a depressing series of forecasts of disastrous events, beginning as follows:

Master, said shee, before that Owes Bridge and Trinitie Church meet, they shall build on the day and it shall fall in the night, untill they get the highest stone of Trinitie Church to be the lowest stone of Owes Bridge, then the day shall come when the North shall rue it wondrous sore, but the South shall rue it for evermore.

This early reference to a North-South divide is worth noting, as it is the very first of the rhymed couplets in which most of the Shipton prophecies are couched. As to its meaning, it seems to be quite unconnected with the Ouse Bridge prophecy, and is one of many isolated predictions of doom – possibly a reference to Henry VIII's suppression of monasteries and religious houses.

This suggested explanation was given by the political astrologer, William Lilly, eagerly quoted by both sides in the Civil War and said to have been 'worth more than half a dozen regiments' by an envious Royalist officer for the way his predictions could raise morale. Lilly published his own edition of Mother Shipton's prophecies only four years after their first known appearance.

His *Ancient and Moderne Prophesies* (1645) contains some useful commentaries and editorial corrections, probably based on information obtained from officers who had been at York around the time of the Battle of Marston Moor, the previous year. He amends incorrect spelling of York street names, for example, and adds snippets culled from local tradition.

The importance of this publication, however, is that the small 1641 edition of Mother Shipton's prophecies might easily have fallen into neglect if it had not been given this kind of endorsement by an astrologer and scholar of the standing of William Lilly, a friend of Elias Ashmole of Oxford. Lilly's version, which sold 4,500 copies, would have the effect of introducing the York prophetess to a wider public, especially as he declared in his Preface: 'Mother Shipton was never yet questioned either for the verity or antiquity; the North of England hath many more of hers'. Thanks to Lilly we have evidence of a definite corpus of Yorkshire prophetic tradition at the early date of 1645.

The prophecy concerning the Ouse Bridge is convincingly local. York people were – and still are – all too familiar with the flooding of the River Ouse, which has often carried away stones from the bridges, especially Ouse Bridge. This has always been an important feature, situated in the middle of the city and carrying major traffic. William Lilly was convinced that Mother Shipton had foreseen this particular damage to the bridge, and the means of its repair. Moreover, he tells us that York people had consciously brought about the fulfilment of her prophecy:

This came to pass, for the Trinity steeple in York was blown down with a tempest, and Owse Bridge was broken down with a great flood, and what they did in repairing the bridge in the day time with the stone of the steeple, fell down in the night, until they [remembering this Prophecy] laid the highest stone of the steeple for the foundation of the bridge; and then the work stood. And by this was fulfilled another of Mother Shipton's prophecies, viz. That her maid should drive her Cowe over Trinity steeple.

The prophecy made by Mother Shipton about her maid-servant and her cow does not appear anywhere else, and must be an item of seventeenth-century Yorkshire folklore preserved by Lilly. If true, of course, it would confirm the impression that Mother Shipton was a

York woman living in comfortable circumstances.

Historical support for Lilly's interpretation of the prophecy is quite strong. Three York churches bore the name of Holy Trinity. The only one of which a collapsed tower is recorded is the church of Holy Trinity Priory, situated just inside the southern walls, near Micklegate Bar. After the dissolution of the monasteries it was used as a parish church, and it is known that in 1551 the central tower fell down.

In the winter of 1564 there was spectacular damage to Ouse Bridge caused by a heavy fall of snow followed by a sudden thaw, with masses of floating ice. Two arches were swept away, along with twelve houses built along the bridge. Twelve people were killed in the disaster. Records refer to a decision to use stone for the repair obtained from a disused manor house, and also from part of a tower in the city wall. There is no documentary reference to stone from Holy Trinity being used, but such economical reusage of material was obviously a common practice, and there is no reason to doubt the story. The two central arches were eventually replaced by a single span of 81 feet, much admired at the time as one of the largest in Europe.

The prophecy of the collapse of the tower and bridge appeared almost eighty years after the event had taken place, so it could be argued that it had been composed in retrospect. Lilly, however, does at least preserve the oral tradition that York people had recalled Mother Shipton's prophecy at the time of the collapse, and had acted upon it by superstitiously incorporating a stone from the top of Trinity Church steeple in the foundation of their repaired bridge.

This local prophecy is linked, by the rhymed comment on the South suffering even more than the North, to a prediction of national calamity, apparently involving widespread famine:

When Hares kindle on cold harth stones, the Lads shall marry Ladyes, and bring them home, then shall you have a yeare of pyning hungar, and then a dearth without Corne; A woful day shall be seen in England, a King and Queene, the first comming of the King of Scots shall be at Holgate Towne, but he shall not come through the barre, and when King of the North shall bee at London Bridge, his Tayle shall be at Edenborough.

Lilly tells us that 'at Lord William Howard's house at Naworth a hare came and kindled (i.e. gave birth) in his kitchen upon the hearth'. This incident must have been remembered because it helped to pinpoint the start of a year of famine, resulting from a failed harvest.

The woeful day associated with a King and Queen probably refers to the unpopular marriage of Mary Tudor to Philip II of Spain in 1554. The 'King of Scots' is undoubtedly James VI of Scotland, who in 1603 became James I of England. Lilly says that this prophecy was fulfilled because when James came to York on the journey to his enthronement in London 'such a multitude of people stood at Holgate Bar to behold him that, to avoid the presse, he was forced to ride another way'.

I have not been able to find historical confirmation of what Lilly states here. Though the new king was acclaimed by the crowds, the official welcome to York seems to have proceeded without any change of plan.

The Royal Progress from Edinburgh to London arrived at York on the 16th April, 1603. King James was received at the east end of Skip Bridge by two city sheriffs, accompanied by a hundred York citizens and sixty gentlemen on horseback, who conducted him to Micklegate Bar.

Here he was welcomed by the Lord Mayor, twelve aldermen in their scarlet robes, and various other dignitaries. The Lord Mayor delivered to the King the sword of state and the keys of the city, then the company processed to the Minster, a canopy being held over the King's head by six lords.

There was a special service with an oration by the Dean in Latin, then James went to stay at the King's Manor. Mother Shipton's reference to the King's tail being in 'Edenborough' (Edinburgh) is said by Lilly to refer to the fact that James's children were waiting there, preparing to follow him to London.

The next prophecy returns to Ouse Bridge. Apparently intrigued by paradoxical novelties, Mother Shipton, having posed the conundrum about her cow been driven over Trinity steeple, now touches on the fact the bridge not only went over the water, but that water also went over the bridge:

After this shall water come over Owes Bridge, and a Windmill shall be set on a Tower, and an Elme-tree shall lye at every mans doore . . .

Lilly elucidates as follows: 'This is verified by the conducting of water into Yorke streets through bored elms, and the conduit-house had a windmill on top that drew up the water'. Historical evidence certainly supports this explanation. The York Corporation records show that in 1616 a Mr. Maltby was employed to supply water by means of wooden conduits or pipes. In 1620 these were laid across Ouse Bridge, 300 trees being bought for the purpose. Though there are references to water being carried in leather bags on horseback, the Shipton allusion is really to the first attempt at a public water-supply 'to every man's door'.

In 1710 and 1711 there are further references to these wooden water-pipes, called 'trees', when it is noted that leakage is damaging the structure of Ouse Bridge.

The next section of the prophecy is much more obscure. 'A time will come', says Mother Shipton, 'when women shall wear great hats and great bands', and a Lord Mayor of York is warned to 'beware of a stab'. Two knights – identified by Lilly as Sir Thomas Wentworth and Sir John Savil – will 'fall out' in Castle Yard. The area known as Colton Hagge will bear crops of corn for seven years, then there will be 'newes' – not specified, but presumably another disaster. Two judges will 'goe in and out at Mungate Bar' (i.e. Monkgate Bar). Lilly says that in 1606 two judges of the York assizes created a precedent by going out by a gate 'where never any judges were known to go out before or since'.

Equally vague, though remarkable for being the very first of Mother Shipton's prophecies to be set out as a separate piece of verse, is the section which follows:

> The Warres shall begin in the spring,
> Much woe to England it shall bring:
> Then shall the Ladyes cry well-away
> That ever we lived to see this day.

Which wars are envisaged? There is the implication that the woe is to befall England alone, so we could read this as a forecast of the Civil War, which broke out in 1642, the year after this prophecy first appeared – or it could refer to the prelude to this, the 'Bishops' War', which had taken place in 1639. In the somewhat confused passage which follows this verse we are told that the war will last three years

– a period which happens to cover the main part of the Roundhead-Cavalier conflict up to Cromwell's defeat of Charles I at the Battle of Naseby in 1645. The prediction continues, partly in rhyme, adding details which can scarcely be applied to the Civil War:

between Cadron (? Calder) and Aire shall be great warfare, when all the world is as a lost, it shall be called Christ's crost, when the battell begins it shall be where Crookbackt Richard made his fray . . .

The last allusion is obviously to Richard III, who was killed at the Battle of Bosworth Field in 1485. Lilly, without using this familiar name of the battle that ended the Wars of the Roses, comments that the site was 'near Leicester', and adds that here Colonel Hastings was one of the first in arms – probably meaning Sir William Hastings, executed by Richard III.

He does not refer to the Battle of Naseby, Cromwell's decisive victory in the Civil War, which took place on the 14th June 1645, the year Lilly's version appeared. Presumably he learnt of this after his book had gone to press. If he had known of it he might have stretched a point by saying that the crucial Battle of Naseby took place where Mother Shipton had predicted, because it also was fought near Leicester, though some twenty miles south-east of the site of Bosworth Field.

Yet Lilly sees an allusion to the Civil War in the prediction which immediately follows Mother Shipton's reference to a battle near Leicester. This runs:

. . . they shall say, To warfare for your King, for halfe a crowne a day, but stirre not (she will say) to warfare for your King, on paine of hanging, but stirre not, for he that goes to complaine, shall not come backe again.

This Lilly sees as a successful prophecy of the fact that in 1642 'Two shillings and sixpence was publickly promised by many Lords for the King's use, to pay one Horseman a day's wages' – no doubt a fact he had picked up through his Royalist military contacts.

Before going on to prophesy further battles Mother Shipton apparently delivered the following cryptic prognostication to Master Besely. Once again it is in rhymed prose:

The time will come when England shall tremble and quake
for feare of a dead man that shall bee hearde to speake,
then will the Dragon give the Bull a great snap,
and when the one is downe they will go to London Towne.

This, understandably, had Lilly baffled, and his only comment was that the prophecy was 'not fulfilled'. Nor has it been since Lilly's day – though it would not be difficult to find instances of reports of posthumous activities, such as ghostly apparitions, resulting in public terror, or to discover topical identifications of a political 'Dragon' and 'Bull'. Prophecies attributed to Merlin had referred to a mysterious 'dead man', variously interpreted as King Arthur and Edward VI. Mother Shipton next forecasts 'a great battell between England and Scotland', successive stages of which will take place at 'Brammammore', 'Knavesmore', and 'Stocknmore'. Lilly could only comment that this predicted war with Scotland was 'not fulfilled'.

Now follows the most bloodthirsty part of all the early predictions attributed to Mother Shipton. The general context could have been suggested by someone anticipating the Civil War, but even the bloody battles of that conflict did not amount to Shipton's slaughter-house spectacular of a whole nation knee-deep in blood. Though obscure, confused and rambling, it is worth quoting this section in full in order to give an idea of the breathless fluency with which it seems to have been delivered, with the prophetess switching the vision from London and the nation to Yorkshire and York:

Then will Ravens sit on the Crosse and drinke as much bloud of the nobles, as of the Commons, then woe is mee, for London shall be destroyed for ever after; Then there shall come a woman with one eye, and she shall tread in many mens bloud to the knee, and a man leaning on a staffe by her, and she shall say to him, What art thou? and he shall say, I am King of the Scots, and she shall say, Goe with me to my house, for there are three Knights, and he will go with her, and stay there three days and three nights, then will England be lost; and they will cry twice of a day England is lost; Then there will be three knights in Petergate in Yorke and the one shall not know of the other; There shall be a childe born in Pomfret with three thumbes, and those three Knights will give him three Horses to hold, while they win England, and all the Noble bloud shall be gone but one, and they shall carry him to Sheriffe Nutton's Castle, six miles from Yorke, and he shall dye there, and they shall choose there an Earle in the field, and hanging their Horses on a thorne, And rue the time that every they were borne, to see so much bloudshed.

Lilly was reduced to silence by this welter of blood, making no attempt at interpretation. He did, however, comment on the three-thumbed prodigy of Pomfret (Pontefract), making the assertion: 'There is a child not many yeares since born at Pomfret with three thumbs'. This curious prediction somehow became incorporated into the 'Cheshire Prophesie' attributed to Robert Nixon (? late fifteenth century) which claimed that 'a boy will be born with three thumbs, and shall hold three king's horses while England shall three times be won and lost in one day'. Evidence that the 'three thumbs' and welter-of-blood prophecies were still current in the mid-eighteenth century is a comment in Fielding's novel *Tom Jones* (1749) by a character who says:

... all the prophecies I have ever read speak of a great deal of blood to be spilt on the ground, and of the miller with three thumbs, who is now alive, and is to hold the horses of three knights up to his knees in blood

Most of the blood-bath prophecies of Mother Shipton remain utterly obscure, including the identity of the one-eyed woman and the reference to Sheriff Hutton (not Nutton, as it was constantly misprinted). They have variously been interpreted as predicting – or, at least, reflecting – the Wars of the Roses, the Civil War, the Revolution of 1688 and the Jacobite Rebellion of 1745.

In contrast to this obscurity, the last section of the 1641 edition of Mother Shipton's prophecies comes so uncannily close to precognition of two precise well-documented historical disasters – the Siege of York and the Fire of London – that these deserve to be examined in a separate chapter.

3

The Siege of York and the Fire of London

What is of immediate interest concerning the Siege of York (1644) and the Great Fire of London (1666) is that both took place at least a century after they were alleged to have been predicted by Mother Shipton, and – from the strictly historical stand-point – three years and twenty-five years respectively after they had appeared in print in the 1641 Lownds Pamphlet. Here, then, is the possibility of showing that Mother Shipton really may have predicted something – as distinct from having had historical events dishonestly woven into the sayings attributed to her.

Mother Shipton's vision of the Siege of York, as apparently given to Reynold Besely, was as follows:

Then they will come to Yorke to besiege it, and they shall keep out three dayes and three nights, and a penny loafe shall bee within the barre at halfe a crowne, and without the barre at a penny; And they will sweare if they will not yeeld, to blow up the Towne walls. Then they will let them in, and they will hang up the Mayor, Sheriffs and Aldermen, and they will goe into Crouch Church; [i.e. St. Crux] there will be three Knights goe in, and but one come out againe; and he will cause Proclamation to be made, that any man may take House, Tower, or Bower for twentie one yeares, and whilest the world endureth, there shall never be warfare againe, nor any more Kings or Queenes, but the Kingdome shall be governed by three Lords, and then York shall be London.

The first part of this prophecy certainly appears to have been fulfilled to the extent that in 1644 there really was a Siege of York, involving both the scarcity of food and the blowing-up of the town walls – the latter an actual occurrence, rather than a threat. The anticipation of such an episode is remarkable enough. What is more remarkable is that no commentator on Mother Shipton – so far as I am aware – has ever noted it as an apparently successful prediction. William Lilly slipped up badly here. His comment simply reads: 'The prophecy of the siege of York and its accompanying antecedents not fulfilled'. This surprising statement can only be explained by Lilly's 1645 version of the prophecies having been sent to the printer before the summer of 1644 – or by Lilly's failure to check whether or not such a siege had occurred. Contemporary York readers of his version of their locally-generated predictions must have been amazed at Lilly's neglect of a rare opportunity to show that Mother Shipton had come very close to hitting the mark.

The facts concerning the Siege of York are as follows. Shortly before the decisive Battle of Marston Moor most of Yorkshire was in the hands of the Royalists. By the April of 1644, however, the Parliamentarian army had taken Selby and moved to the outskirts of York to join an army from Scotland, with whom there was now an alliance. These armies set up positions within a mile of the walls of York on both sides of the Ouse. They were joined on the 3rd June by troops commanded by Oliver Cromwell and the Earl of Manchester, who camped to the North-east of the city, so that now the whole of York was invested. There were about 5,000 soldiers in the city, but something like 30,000 in the besieging armies.

Though the siege lasted far longer than Mother Shipton's 'three dayes and three nights', there was certainly a scarcity of food in York, especially in the later stages, when rationing was introduced for both civilians and soldiers by the Royalist commander, the Marquis of Newcastle. We can well imagine that a precious loaf of bread would have cost thirty times more 'within the barre' – that is, inside the walls of the besieged city – than it would outside.

The prediction of the threats to 'blow up the Towne walls' proved true enough – but it was an understatement. The Parliamentarians bombarded Skeldersgate, mined St. Mary's Tower, and breached the town walls by using gunpowder, leaving them badly damaged. There were a number of skirmishes, in particular the Parliamentarians' raid on the King's Manor, which they briefly held before retreating, leaving behind 50 dead and 250 prisoners.

In order to relieve the York garrison, Prince Rupert, nephew to Charles I, marched north from Shrewsbury, reaching Knaresborough Castle by the end of June. His army was small compared with the combined Parliamentarian forces, and numbered no more than 14,000. Yet such was Prince Rupert's reputation that all opposition fled before him – except for the armies associated with Cromwell, who responded by moving out from York to block the advancing Royalist army at Marston Moor, near Tockwith. At first Prince

Rupert's troops out-manoevred them by marching north-east through Boroughbridge and on to York, where they lifted the siege for a day or two. In the final conflict at Marston Moor, however, which came in the evening of the 2nd July, the Royalists, after two hours of bloody battle, were overwhelmingly defeated. The Siege of York was resumed by the Parliamentarians, and only a fortnight later, on the 16th July, the garrison surrendered.

The Mother Shipton prediction is of a besieged York which surrenders in order to avoid having the walls blown up. This was obviously inaccurate in that the garrison continued to resist in spite of bombardment and damage to the walls.

The predicted surrender – 'then they will let them in' – came about, not because of threats, but because of the hopelessness of the situation, a handful of Royalist troops, many wounded at Marston Moor, now being surrounded by the victorious armies of Cromwell. The remnant of Royalist soldiers – scarcely more than a thousand – were allowed to march out of York with honour and with colours flying.

Even less successful was the prediction that the victorious besiegers would execute the Mayor, Sheriffs and Aldermen. There is no record of any official being hanged at this time, and eventually in 1647, the Lord Mayor, Thomas Dickinson, took over the civic leadership quite peacefully from Lord Fairfax. It is significant, incidentally, that though in some measure Mother Shipton foresaw the siege of York, she made no mention of the siege and capture of Knaresborough Castle by the Parliamentarians led by John Lilburne a few months later, in December 1644.

The nearest Mother Shipton came to the political reality that followed the decisive turning-point of Marston Moor was her vision of the country being governed by lords rather than by royalty – a description which surely applied when Charles I had been beheaded and Cromwell ruled as Lord Protector. The prediction that there would not be 'any more Kings or Queens' would certainly have been seen as amply fulfilled by people living during the Commonwealth (1649-60). The limitation of this prophecy of future republicanism is that Mother Shipton mistakingly sees it as a permanent state of affairs, linked with a golden age of universal peace.

Alas, there is still no sign of the fulfilment of her prediction – a pleasant contrast to her bloodthirsty utterances – that 'whilest the world endureth, there shall never be warfare again'.

Nor can any historical situation be found to correspond to her forecast of an unprecedented shortage of men, presumably as a result of so many having been slaughtered in the successive battles she had predicted. Only women, she tells us, will be left to gather in the harvest, and men will become so scarce that a girl who sees one will rush home to tell her mother:

And after this shall be a white Harvest of corne gotten in by women. Then shall be in the North, that one woman shall say unto another, Mother I have seen a man to day, and for one man there shall be a thousand women; there shall be a man sitting upon St. James's Church hill weeping his fill . . .

The ratio of one man to a thousand women could well be regarded as a delightful predicament from the man's point of view – so this does not seem to have any logical connection with a mystery-man who will be 'weeping his fill', and this is probably to intoduce the concluding disaster we shall shortly consider.

The prediction about the extreme scarcity of men became sufficiently well known for a large oil-painting to have been made depicting it. Dating from the middle of the eighteenth century, it was for many years on display in the Crown and Woolpack Inn on the Great North Road, near Stilton.

It featured a solitary gentleman, surrounded by affectionate women, one of whom was saying, according to the bubble-caption, 'Oh, mother! I see a man'. Peering malevolently over their shoulders was Mother Shipton, 'with a most forbidding expression on her hooked features'. As far away as Norfolk, in the parish of Irstead, there was a strong oral tradition of Mother Shipton's prophecies, the version of the relevant one being recorded in the last century as follows:

The men are to be killed, so that one man shall be left to seven women; and the daughters shall come home and say to their mothers: 'Lawk, Mother! I have seen a man'. The women shall have to finish the harvest.

Whatever was meant by this forecast of a widespread dearth of men, there is no doubt that the final part of the 1641 prophecy referred to a disaster that was to overtake London.

It was to be so severe that hardly any houses would be left standing.

There is no mention of the cause, and certainly no hint of fire, yet this prophecy – supplemented by other traditions – was considered by the Londoners of 1666 to have been Mother Shipton's reference to the Great Fire of that year. The concluding part of the 1641 Lownds Pamphlet is as follows:

And after that a Ship come sayling up the Thames till it come against London, and the Master of the Ship shall weepe, and the Marriners shall aske him why hee weepeth, being he hath made so good a voyage, and he shall say; Ah what a goodly Citie this was, none in the world comparable to it, and now there is scarce left any house that can let us have drinke for our money.

> Unhappy he that lives to see these days,
> But happy are the dead Shiptons wife sayes.

A couplet which did not appear in print until 1667, but which may have been preserved from an earlier tradition, was also interpreted as Mother Shipton's forecast of both the Plague of 1665 and the Fire which followed it:

> Triumphant death rides London through
> And men on tops of Houses go.

A commentary on these lines by Richard Head, who first published them, can be taken as typical of the general view of his day, even though Head was a fanciful and unreliable writer, always to be read with caution:

This was suddenly fulfilled in the great Conflagration of Fire, which happened in London, Sept. 2,3 and 4, Anno 1666, by which so many houses were destroyed that men afterwards in the Ruines, went on the tops of those Houses, whose lofty structures not long before, seemed to brave the skie, and which would dazle weak eyes to look up and behold the tops of them.

Head supplemented this with another verse which he asserted had been uttered by Mother Shipton, the vision being of an age of prosperity following the devastation of the Great Fire:

40

The Fiery Year as soon as o're,
Peace shall then be as before,
Plenty every where is found,
And Men with Swords shall plow the Ground.

By the eighteenth century the statement that Mother Shipton had prophesied both the Plague and the Fire was being made with great confidence. In a 1743 edition, for example, we find the following commentary on the 'Triumphant Death' and 'Tops of Houses' couplet:

The first, in all Appearance, points out the terrible Plague that raged in London in 1665, which carried off in a little Time, in London only, 68,566 Souls. The second circumstantially alludes to the dreadful Fire in the Year following, when 13,000 Houses were consumed to Ashes; signifying that People should be obliged to run from one House to another, over the Tops of the Houses, to save themselves and their Effects.

This same writer gives a slightly different version of the passage about the ship's captain. This may well be from a parallel tradition, though it could simply be an edited version of the 1641 printed prophecy:

Time shall happen a Ship shall sail upon the River Thames, 'till it reach the City of London, the Master shall weep, and cry out, Ah! What a flourishing City was this when I left it! Unequalled through the World! But now scarce a House is left to entertain us with a Flaggon.

Whether or not these passages are seen by a modern reader as prophecy of the Great Fire there is good evidence that Shipton traditions of this kind were firmly believed by those who saw the Fire in 1666.

Samuel Pepys, the observant naval administrator and diarist, has preserved an interesting testimony to the fact that the ship's captain prophecy was so well-known that it was immediately seen as applicable. He recorded on the 20th October 1666 that he was taking a walk with Commissioner Middleton, an authority on the Royal Navy, who had just returned from Portsmouth. Referring to Middleton, he wrote:

41

He says he was on board The Prince when the newes came of the burning of London; and all the Prince said was, that now Shipton's prophecy was out.

This is complicated by the fact that two Princes are to be distinguished. The first refers to the ship, the second (as Pepys commentators suggest) refers to Prince Rupert, who had fought at Marston Moor after raising the Siege of York, and had possibly come across Mother Shipton's prophecies when in Yorkshire. It is significant, though, that Pepys gives no explanation of who 'Shipton' is, the implication being that the name was perfectly familiar to his readers. This is supported by the observation of Daniel Defoe in his *Journal of the Plague Year* that in the 1660s the 'sign of Mother Shipton' was a common sight outside the homes of London fortune-tellers.

At the time of the Plague, and especially when it was succeeded by the Fire of the following year, public interest naturally concentrated on the Shipton prophecy of a London disaster. It is alluded to in letters of the period, such as one written to Viscount Scudamore on the 6th September, 1666, which shows that belief in Mother Shipton's power to foretell the future was strong enough to lead thousands of ordinary people to take a fatalistic attitude to the Great Fire. The conviction that it was inevitable, because infallibly predicted, only added to the chaos:

All orders signified nothing . . . The city, for the first rank, they minded only their own preservation; the middle sort [were] so distracted and amazed that they did not know what they did; the poorer, they minded nothing but pilfering; so the city [was] abandoned to the fire and thousands believing in Mother Shipton's prophecy 'That London in Sixty-six should be burnt to ashes'.

No surviving version of Mother Shipton's prophecies is specific enough to give the year (16)66 or to refer to London being burnt to ashes. It therefore seems to me very likely that, since Mother Shipton was sometimes linked with Nostradamus, her predictions about London may have been confused with these lines attributed to the French prophet:

> Le sang du juste a Londres fera faute
> Brulez par foudres, de vingt trois six..

The blood of the righteous will be taken in London,
Burnt by fire from heaven in three twenties plus six.

In addition to Nostradamus various English astrologers were supposed to have predicted the Great Fire, in particular, William Lilly. No doubt influenced by the Shipton material he had published, he decided to look into the question of future disasters himself, and in *Monarchy or No Monarchy* (1651) wrote of 'a catastrophe . . . ominous to London . . . by reason of sundry fires and a consuming plague'. In his own copy he had written under the woodcut illustrating the fire, 'expected in 1693 . . . or perhaps 1666 or 1667'. This was near enough for Lilly to be brought before a special committee on suspicion of his actually having started the fire himself in order to make his forecast come true and thereby gain much credit.

Notwithstanding Lilly, Nostradamus and the rest, the prediction of the Great Fire was attributed by many Londoners to Mother Shipton, either because of the 1641 Lownds Pamphlet, or the later 'Tops of Houses' prediction, or a variant of the latter, though as this refers so plainly to the Restoration of Charles II, it is considerably suspect:

When fate to England shall restore
A king to reign as heretofore,
Great death in London shall be through
And many houses be laid low.

We can take it that this and similar prophetic verses were composed in retrospect. But there is still sufficient evidence to prove an early oral tradition about Mother Shipton and the Fire. This itself could be regarded as no more than the superstition of the ignorant crowds, desperate to find some explanation for the catastrophe. But such a view is not really tenable when we consider that 'Shipton's prophecy' was apparently taken seriously by such well-educated men as Pepys, Prince Rupert and Viscount Scudamore.

There can be no doubt that, in whatever form the prophecy was circulating, there were very many Londoners in 1666 who – according to one eye-witness account – were so sure that Mother Shipton had predicted the fire that they 'refused to make any efforts to prevent it . . . for it was written in the great book of fate that

London was to be destroyed. Hundreds of persons who might have rendered valuable assistance, and saved whole parishes from devastation, folded their arms and looked on'.

Yet although contemporary Londoners reacted in this way there is insufficient evidence for a modern researcher to give full support to the glib, much-repeated, much-copied statement that 'Mother Shipton prophesied the Fire of London'. If the Londoners of 1666 had access to a detailed prophecy about fire and ashes, we have not. All we have is a general statement of widespread destruction, with no hint of a conflagration in the prophecies printed before the Great Fire.

Even so, the following facts are worthy of note. The famous fire destroyed 13,200 houses, including shops, inns and ale-houses, caused ten million pounds of damage and left about 100,000 people homeless. Place beside these facts Mother Shipton's vision of a devastated London, where there was 'scarce left any house', and it must be conceded that she was by no means wide of the mark.

So it would be reasonable to conclude that, both in the case of the Siege of York and the Fire of London prophecies attributed to Mother Shipton, and printed before those events took place, come intriguingly close to describing future disasters that were to befall these two great cities.

The 'Mother Shipton' Moth

4

An Irish Pornographer's Mother Shipton

Most of the nonsense that has been talked and written about Mother
Shipton – right until the present day – is uncritically derived from
Richard Head's leg-pull of a chapbook *The Life and Death of Mother
Shipton*, apparently first published in London in 1667. The difficulty
about dating Head's work is that the earliest known copy (in the
British Library) is dated 1684. The title-page, however, refers to
'this present year 1667', and a play derived from Head was published
in 1668 – so we can take it that his chapbook first appeared in 1667,
the year following the Great Fire, when the time was ripe to exploit
Mother Shipton as the supernaturally-gifted witch who had allegedly
foretold it.

This date, 179 years after the supposed birth of the prophetess,
immediately strikes us as far too late to provide a reliable source,
especially as it purports to give us facts about Mother Shipton – the
statement that she was born in Knaresborough, her mother's
Christian name, the latter's seduction by the Devil, and so forth –
which are not even hinted at in any earlier writing. Even so, though
Head had clearly never set foot in Knaresborough, it remains
possible that he had picked up local traditions by talking to people in
London who had been staying in this historic town, which in the
Restoration period was a popular centre for 'taking the waters'.
Then known as 'The Knaresborough Spaw' it was a useful base for
visiting not only its own petrifying Dropping Well but the mineral
springs some three miles away, which were being developed as the
major new spa of Harrogate. As thousands were now flocking to this
area every summer it is possible that Head saw the prospect of a
good market amongst the spa visitors for a saucy chapbook about a
local character.

Richard Head was born in Ireland in about 1637, probably at
Carrickfergus, near Belfast, where his father was murdered in 1641.
He came to England to spend a brief period at the University of
Oxford before attempting to earn his living as a bookseller in Little
Britain, London. Having got into serious debt through gambling, he

fled back to Ireland, where he led a poverty-stricken life in Dublin. He eventually returned to London to start a bookshop again, but he was ruined by further gambling, and became notorious for his wild and dissolute life. His contemporary, John Aubrey, wrote of him in *Brief Lives*:

> He had been among the gypsies. He looked like a knave, with his goggling eyes. He could transforme himselfe into any shape. Broke 2 or 3 times. He maintained himselfe by scribling. He got 20s. per sheet.

Aubrey adds that Head was drowned when he was crossing to the Isle of Wight. He was then aged fifty, which would mean that he died in about 1687, the year of the third edition of his little book on Mother Shipton.

Richard Head (? 1637 – 1687),
who 'looked like a knave, with his goggling eyes',
Salacious author of The Life and Death of Mother Shipton

Head's only well-known work is the picaresque novel *The English Rogue* (1665), a semi-autobiographical tale reflecting the author's salaciousness in ale-house and bawdy-house. At first it was an under-the-counter book, regarded as soft porn by seventeenth-century standards, with the copies printed and sold secretly, circulating in inns and brothels.

It was submitted to the Censors of the Press, but they refused a licence on account of its obscenity. Eventually publication was allowed after Head had removed the most offensive parts. What remains is lively vulgarity, and a convincing account of rogues, pimps and prostitutes.

Although *The English Rogue* has been reprinted in modern times, most of Head's other works survive only as rare items in such libraries as the Bodleian and the British Library. There is, for example, *The Canting Academy* (1674), which confirms Aubrey's remark that Head had lived amongst the gypsies. This is a collection of tales about gypsies, fortune-tellers, rogues, swindlers and the criminal underworld in general. As Head's later version of Mother Shipton contains many rhymed couplets alleged to be her prophecies, it is worth showing that he had a facility for knocking out light verse. In *The Canting Academy* we find, for example, a poem which he claims to be in the cant or slang used by criminals, which opens:

> The Rogue's delight in praise of his Strolling Mort.
> Doxy, oh! Thy Glaziers shine
> As Glymmar by the Salomon;
> No Gentry Mort hath parts like thine,
> No Cove e're wap'd with such a one!

Head translates this as follows:

> My Honey Chuck, by the Mass I swear,
> Thine eyes do shine than fire more clear;
> No silken Girl hath thighs like thine,
> No Doe was ever buck'd like mine!

This book contains frankly pornographic verse, a chapter on 'The Bawd, Pimp and Whore', and – though most of it is frivolous – there is perhaps a serious contribution in the concluding item, a

'Canting Dictionary' of terms for crimes and vices.

Aubrey's comment that Head was a scribbler, quickly producing material for booksellers at a sovereign a sheet, is confirmed by his other books and pamphlets. In 1675 he published *Roteus Redivivus or the Art of Wheedling or Insinuation*, a book of practical advice for the would-be con-man. Similarly unedifying was his *Nugae Venales or a Complaisant Companion* (1686), a collection of jokes, many of them vulgar, and few of them funny by modern standards. Another Latin title, *Hic et Ubique*, was given to his comedy *The Humours of Dublin* (1663), which was 'acted privately, with general Applause'. His small book *The Floating Island* (1673) is an account of an imaginary, fantastic journey, written in typical tongue-in-cheek style.

In order to evaluate Head's version of Mother Shipton it is essential to see it in the context of his other writing. As an author he could fairly be described as lively and original, but so inclined to sensationalism, fantasy and downright deception, to say nothing of his fondness for Restoration ribaldry, that he can rarely be taken at face value.

To the discerning reader, Richard Head's *The Life and Death of Mother Shipton* is immediately seen as a playful fake. A note on the title-page claims that Head is presenting to the public newly-discovered details concerning Mother Shipton:

Being not only an Account of the strange Birth, the most important Passages of her life; but also her Prophesies, now newly Collected . . . Strangely preserved amongst other writings belonging to an old Monastry in York-shire, and now Published for the information of Posterity.

In a quaint foreword, addressed to his 'Beloved Countrymen', the author disappoints us by not revealing the identity of this Yorkshire monastery, but claims it had been given by Henry VIII to a gentleman who had in his keeping some 'ancient Writings' found here. It was, incidentally, already a familiar trick to pretend that prophecies had been found in some old building, especially a monastery, as monks were popularly believed to have mysterious, occult powers. In 1677 a non-conformist minister, the Rev Richard Gilpin, remarked that 'an old prophecy, pretended to be found in a wall or taken out of an old manuscript . . . is usually more doted on than the plain and infallible rules of Scripture'.

The ancient writings found in this unnamed Yorkshire monastery were, Head tells us, unfortunately 'so injured by Time, as now not legible to read'. Undaunted, he persuaded the owner to let him borrow the manuscript, he claims, and then, in the manner of an alchemist, he set about its restoration:

I took of the best Galls I could get, beat them grosly, and laid them to steep one day in good white-wine, that done, I distilled them with the Wine; and with the distilled Water that came off them, I wetted handsomly the old Letters whereby they seemed as fresh and fair, as if they had been but newly written; here did I find her Life and Prophesies copied out by an impartial hand, which I have in this book presented to thy view.

The chemical process he describes is not far-fetched. There is no doubt that galls (from oak-trees) contain tannic acid, from which ink can be made and which has the property of darkening faded writing. A curious example of this, in fact, can be seen in Knaresborough in the Parish Register, started in 1561.

Many names have been obliterated, especially around the time of the Civil War. Locally believed to have been vandalism by Cromwell's soldiers, it is likely that these names were ones that had faded, and were then brought out with gallic fluid, which has since blackened with age.

Having button-holed his reader with this intriguing picture of an ancient manuscript yielding its secrets, Head is now in a position to write what he likes. On reading his draft for the printer, however, it seems to have occurred to him that he might have gone too far in his invention. At the end of the foreword he adds this 'Postscript':

Courteous Reader, let me desire thee Candidly to pass Over some seeming Impossibilities in the first sheet [allowing the Author Licentia Poetica in her description] and some Actions performed in her Minority, and only to weigh the more serious part of her Prophesies . . .

Head's account is printed – in the first surviving edition of 1684 – in already outmoded gothic 'black-letter' type, to give it an air of antiquity. He opens it in the manner of an ordinary biographer, informing us that in 1486 there lived a girl called Agatha Shipton 'at a place called Naseborough near the Dropping-Well in York-shire'.

Mother Shipton looking back to when her teenage mother,
Agatha, is seduced by the Devil in disguise.
(Frontispiece of Richard Head's publications, 1667, 1687)

At the age of fifteen this girl was left an orphan, and though she 'still inhabited in the old House', she soon became destitute. After only a few lines of sober narrative Head starts to spin his fairy-tale. .

One day, he tells us, the Devil approached young Agatha when she was 'sitting Melancholy under a Tree by a River side'. Because

Head has no knowledge of Knaresborough whatever, he does not even set the scene on '*the* river' (i.e. the River Nidd), on which the town is built. The Devil appeared to the girl in the form of a 'very handsome man', magnificently apparelled, and offered to help her. Not suspecting that a Devil 'hid in that comely shape', Agatha told him of her poverty . . . 'Pish (said the Devil) this is nothing. Be ruled by me, and all shall be well'. Having announced that he intended to marry her, the Devil arranged to meet her the next day at the same place. He duly arrived, 'riding upon a stately Horse with a pillion behind him for his Spouse', and accompanied by gallants, 'his Divel-ships attendants', who helped him to carry the girl off with supernatural speed. They arrived at a fairy palace where Agatha was clothed in rich garments and ushered into a banqueting hall, where the table was 'furnished with all the varieties the whole world could afford'. With the food they had the choicest wines and the sweetest music . . .

Dinner being ended, they fell to Dancing; and now could my lecherous Divil stay no longer, but he must needs walk a corant with his Mistris into another private room, and there courted her to lust; the simple Girl consented, and so they both went to bed together, with the Ceremonies of Marriage. His touches (as she confessed to the Midwife that delivered her of her Devilish Offspring) were as cold as ice or snow.

In this passage Head blends prurience with folklore. The notion of the Devil's sexual touches being experienced as ice-cold was very widespread, and can be found both in folk-tales and reports of witch-trials.

The Devil now tells Agatha that he will equip her to become a witch, sharing with her some of his evil secrets and arts – details of which Head could easily have drawn from contemporary traditions about witchcraft, reports of witch-trials and even Shakespeare's witches in *Macbeth*, with their spine-chilling supernatural powers, including accurate prophecy:

. . . I can when I please pierce through the Earth and ransack its Treasures . . . I know all rare Arts and Sciences and can teach them to whom I please. I can disturb the Element, stir up Thunders and Lightnings . . . and can appear in what shape or form I please . . . I will give thee power to raise Haile, Tempests, with Lightning and Thunder, the winds shall be at thy command . . . Thou shalt, moreover, heal or kill whom thou pleasest; destroy or preserve either man or beast; know what is past, and assuredly tell what is to come.

Head's description of the Devil's initiation of the fifteen-year old witch is clearly a piece of cynical nonsense, with its extravagant, contrived gibberish, containing hints of the conjuration of evil spirits. Typical of Head, he does not miss the opportunity to include the sexual connotation of the 'witch-pap', so frequently mentioned in witch-trials as the means whereby witches suckled their 'familiars' – cats, dogs, monkeys and so forth, regarded as materialisations of the Devil:

Whereupon he bid her say after him, in this manner:

> RazielellimibammirammishziragiaPfonthonp;hanchia
> Raphaelelhaverunatapinotambecazmitzphecat jarid cuman
> hapheah Gabriel Heydon turris dungeonis philonomstarkes
> sophecord bankim. After she had repeated these words after
> him, he pluckt her by the Groin, and there immediately
> grew a kind of Tet, which he instantly suckt, telling her that
> must be his constant Custom with her morning and
> evening; now did he bid her say after him agin, Kametzad
> tuphOdelPharaz TumbaginGall Flemmngrn Victow
> Denmarkeonto.

The gibberish of these incantations defies translation, though scraps of Greek and Latin can be detected, and even perhaps Romany and Turkish. Names of angelic powers are there, such as Gabriel and Raziel. 'Heydon' probably refers to the astrologer John Heydon, arrested in 1663 for declaring that Charles II was a tyrant.

As soon as Agatha is initiated as a witch there is a tremendous thunderstorm, the fairy palace and her fine clothes instantly disappear, and she is transported to a sunless wood. Then two 'flaming fiery Dragons' appear, pulling a chariot. The girl is placed in this and 'with speed unimaginable conveyed through the Air to her own poor cottage'.

Head devotes the next two chapters to Agatha's development as a witch. Her neighbours are shocked to see the change in her appearance, for she now looks '*as if a Hagg had rid her*'. Frequently visited by the Devil, in the guise of the same handsome, lecherous youth, she experiences hallucinations and trances. One day her inquisitive neighbours, who now 'verily believed she was a witch', are hoisted high into the air by a sudden wind:

falling to the ground again without the least harm, only some shame to the women, for they descended with their heads downwards . . . their lower parts appearing all naked to the astonished spectators: the men were seen like overgrown Goats with large horns on their heads, and women riding on their backs.

This kind of writing, though obviously fictional, nevertheless reflects various popular superstitions concerning witchcraft. We see this especially in Head's account of how Agatha took revenge on her critical neighbours, causing mischief to their persons, their cattle and their horses, one of which suddenly died, its opened stomach being found to contain 'fish-hooks and hair instead of hay and oats'.

The account of witchcraft phenomena is spiced by Head with coarse humour based on bodily functions. He tells us, for example, that Agatha took revenge on a dignitary sitting 'with persons of good quality at dinner-time' by supernaturally placing a lavatory seat round his neck where his ruff had been. A man sitting next to him, who thought this amusing, suddenly found his hat replaced by 'the Pan of a Close-stool' (i.e. a lavatory bowl). Head continues:

A modest young Gentlewoman which did sit at the Table at that time, and was come on no other errand but to see this young witch which was so much talked of; looking on these two worthy spectacles of laughter, endeavoured all she could to refrain laughing, but could not, and withall continued farting for above a quarter of an hour.

After witnessing such impressive phenomena as these, the people of the town are convinced that Agatha Shipton is 'the greatest witch in the world', and determine to bring her before the local magistrate. Two men pluck up sufficient courage to enter her house, which is crawling with 'Toads, Adders and such like noisome creatures'. Brought before the judge, she tells him he has no power to detain her, utters three magic words and is carried away by 'a horrid winged Dragon'.

Soon Agatha is seen to be pregnant – and Head's use of the phrase 'the great swelling of her Belly' probably reflects the folk belief that women who had been seduced by the Devil were abnormally large. Anne Ashby of Cranbrook, for example, who was hanged as a witch in 1652, confessed that the Devil had 'known her carnally' and it was observed that 'she swelled into a monstrous and vast bigness'.

The people of the town at first find it difficult to believe that this is the explanation for Agatha's pregnancy, and remark that: 'None would be so vile and wicked as to have Copulation with a Devil incarnate' . . . Agatha is brought before another magistrate, but is released on bail by two mysterious strangers.

Head now makes the most of the supernatural birth of Agatha's diabolical daughter, the famed Mother Shipton. It takes place in the house (not a cave) that the girl had inherited from her parents. The midwife and other women are terrified by the accompanying 'strange and horrible noises' and shocked by the monstrous ugliness of the child, 'so misshapen, that it is altogether impossible to express it fully in words'. Even so, Head does his best, giving us an exuberant description of the child's phenomenal repulsiveness:

. . . very morose and big bon'd, her head very long, with very great goggling, but sharp and fiery eyes, her nose of an incredible and unproportionable length, having in it many crooks and turnings, adorned with many strange Pimples of divers colours, as red, blew, and mixt, which like Vapours of Brimstone gave such a lustre to her affrighted spectators in the dead time of the Night, that one of them confest several times in my hearing, that her Nurse needed no other light to assist her in the performance of her duty; Her Cheeks were of a black swarthy Complexion, much like a mixture of the Black and yellow jaundies; wrinkled, shrivelled and very hollow . . .

Remember that this is what Mother Shipton is supposed to have looked like *when she was born*! The absurd notion of luminous pimples had already been used by Head in *The English Rogue*, where he writes of a man 'whose very face would have enlightened the room, though in the darkest night', as it looked like a blazing comet, the tail being his nose, miraculously still intact in spite of the pox. Head also makes use of folklore again, telling us that the baby was born with a full set of teeth – a traditional sign of a witch – and that they, moreover, seemed like tusks. The portrait continues:

Her Chin was the same complexion as her Face, turning up towards her mouth
. . . Her Neck so strangely distorted, that her right shoulder was forced to be a
supporter to her head, it being propt up by the help of her Chin, in such sort
that the right side of her body stood much lower than her left; like the reeling
of a Ship that failes with a side winde. Again, her left side was quite turned the
contrary way, as if her body had been screw'd together piece after piece.

The infant witch is soon discovered to be even more
supernaturally gifted than her mother, and she terrifies her nurse and
the neighbours by producing weird noises ('as if it had been a
consort of Catts') and, like her mother, causes the menfolk to have
objects descend upon their necks, accompanied by visions of a naked
old woman, hanging upside down. The women are thrown 'flat upon
their bellies, their clothes being turned backwards over their heads,
two great black Catts playing Hocus Pocus on their posteriors . . .'
When the men release the women from the attention of the devil-cats
they are compelled to dance around 'carrying upon every one of their
shoulders an Imp in the likeness of a Monkey or Ape, which hung
close upon them' – an obvious allusion to a witch's familiar, and
probably the origin of the eighteenth-century picture showing Mother
Shipton with a monkey.

The town is now in such an uproar that a delegation led by the
parson goes to Mother Shipton's house. On entering they hear the
child crying 'in a most hideous and dolefull manner', then the sound
of people walking over stones, then harmonious music – and finally
they discover the child in its cradle, suspended in mid-air, three yards
up the chimney. Again, Head here has probably incorporated an
example of the levitation mentioned in witch-trials, such as that of
Jane Brooks of Shepton Mallet (1658), who is said to have levitated
a boy of twelve, keeping him suspended two or three feet above the
floor.

As if this were not nonsense enough Head opens his next chapter
with a crowning absurdity. We recall his catalogue of the child's
horrific disfigurements at birth, then see how he excels himself by
saying: 'Mother Shipton now grew apace, and as her stature
increased, so did her deformity'! He tells us that now 'her supposed
Father (the foul fiend) omitted not a day wherein he visited not the

House . . . sometimes visibly in the form of a Cat, Dog or Hog'. Head would have come across various contemporary references to the power of the Devil to transmogrify himself. Only two years earlier than his publication the Rev. Joseph Glanville had dealt with the various guises of Satan and his power to assume mortal shape in his *Saducismus Triumphatus* (1682). Edward Fairfax of Fewston, in the Forest of Knaresborough, had in his observations on local witches (between 1621 and 1623) described how the Devil had appeared as the vicious 'black cat Gibbe' and other creatures, and had 'changed himself into sundry shapes'. If we are to believe Aubrey, Head had the reputation of being able to do this himself.

With the Devil's assistance Mother Shipton develops amazing powers. Head describes how she can drop through the roof of her house, stretch herself to be taller than any person living, and provoke various poltergeist phenomena, such as have chairs and stools march up and down the stairs, or remove food from under the nose of her nurse.

Left to the care of the Parish (there is no further reference to her mother) she is sent to school, where 'to the amazement and astonishment of her Mistris, she exactly pronounced every letter in the Alphabet without teaching'. Such precociousness naturally makes the other children envious and hostile, some mocking her 'for her monstrous long Nose'. The schoolgirl Mother Shipton takes revenge by pinching them invisibly or striking them dumb – and is soon expelled.

At this point Head seems to lose interest in providing biographical details. He simply says that Mother Shipton, who often talked to herself or burst out laughing for no reason, and used to speak in strange riddles, was now being consulted by people who came from far and wide. The implication is that she was consulted as a fortune-teller in Knaresborough – though the town is not mentioned after the first page. The chapbook ends by saying that she died in York, but offers no explanation as to how she came to be there.

Head next turns his attention to the prophecies he claims to have been uttered by Mother Shipton, now famous 'for her notable Judgement in things to come':

There resorted to her House a number of people of all sorts, both old and young, rich and poor; Especially of the female Sex, viz. Young Maids and Wenches, who have alwaies a great Itching desire to know when they shall be married.

Mother Shipton, he says, was never mercenary, but her maid always made sure that money was handed over after each consultation. On one occasion the maid, rather than lose the opportunity of cash, made up a prophecy herself for a young man anxious to know whether his sick father would die, so he could be sure of his inheritance:

> The Grave provided hath a Room
> Prepare for Death, thy Hour is Come

The son's delight at this news turned to despair when he saw his father make a good recovery – and the prophecy was fulfilled by the death of the son.

The rest of the prophecies given by Head are of a political nature, the first being delivered to a young officer who comes to consult 'our Northern Prophetess' to discover whether or not he should go to war for Henry VIII. In symbolic and convoluted language she predicts a victory over the French, but the passage is of interest because – though Head surprisingly makes no reference to the prediction that Wolsey would never reach York – he does have Mother Shipton declaring this of Wolsey:

> Now shall the Mitred Peacock first begin to plume, whose
> Train shall make a great show in the World, for a time; but
> shall afterwards vanish away, and his great Honour come to
> nothing; which shall take its end at Kingston.

In the lengthy commentary which follows, Head says that when Wolsey heard this prophecy he refused ever to pass through the town of Kingston, and that when he was arrested for high treason by Northumberland and Sir Anthony Kingston (the Lieutenant of the Tower of London) 'his very name (remembering the Prophesie) struck such terror to his heart that he soon after expired'.

Although apparently unfamiliar with the 1641 Lownds Pamphlet, except perhaps through some oral version, Head gives what reads like a garbled account of the secret visit to Mother Shipton's house by Besely and the three lords in disguise. He says that she was visited by 'the Abbot of Beverly', disguised as a layman. There is clearly an echo of the 1641 Pamphlet. Instead of 'Come in, Master Besley' we have 'Come in, Mr. Abbot', followed by a reference to Mother Shipton's ability to see through a disguise.

The difficulty here is that no contemporary 'Abbot of Beverly' is known to history. The monastery which later became Beverley Minster had only three known abbots (704 - 752 AD), and from the eleventh century up to the period of Mother Shipton's alleged prophecy the senior priest was always known as the Provost of Beverley, while the nearby Abbey of Meaux had an Abbot. So his 'Abbot of Beverly' is probably no more than a corruption of the original 'Master Besley' – possibly influenced by 'the Abbot of Bewerley' (further up Nidderdale, near Pateley Bridge), a title sometimes applied to Marmaduke Huby of Fountains Abbey.

The simple device of looking back on some historical incident, composing a bogus prophecy about it, then following it with notes to show how accurate it was, is one that Head exploits to the full. All the predictions he puts into the mouth of Mother Shipton concern events which had already taken place by the time of his publication in 1667. Here is a selection of the rhymed prophecies which he asserts were spoken to the abbot during his second visit. In each case Head's identification is briefly given. In the pamphlet his notes are copious and detailed, occupying far more space than the prophecies, and show an extensive and mostly accurate knowledge of English history:

> A vertuous Lady then shall die
> For being raised up too high.
> > (Lady Jane Grey, executed in 1554)

> The Lyon fierce being dead and gone
> A Maiden Queen shall Reign anon
> > ('Bloody Mary' succeeded by Queen Elizabeth)

> The Western Monarchs Wooden Horses
> Shall be destroyed by the Drakes forces
> > (The Spanish Armada, defeated in 1588)

58

> More wonders yet! a widowed Queen
> In England shall be headless seen
>> (Mary, Queen of Scots, beheaded in 1587)

> Hell's Power by a fatal Blow
> Shall seek the Land to overthrow
>> (The Gunpowder Plot of 1605)

These last lines, Head tells us, 'have reference to the horrid Powder Plot, which was to have been acted by some desperate Papists . . .' He then gives the names of all the conspirators, a detailed account of the stacking of the 36 barrels of gunpowder, the letter to Lord Mounteagle and the arrest of 'Guido Fox'. The abbot was apparently impressed by these prophecies, though at first he had considered them 'like the Oracles at Delphos [which] brought one into a Labyrinth of confused conjectures . . .'

In the midst of her recital of future English history Mother Shipton abruptly stopped, Head tells us, and gave a deep sigh, 'the tears trickling down her cheeks, accompanied with the wringing of her hands'. When asked why she was so distressed she replied: 'Ah, Mr. Abbot . . . Who can with dry eyes repeat what must next ensue, or but think upon it without a heart full of Agony'. Whereupon she unburdened herself of a short prophecy ending with the lines:

> The White King then [O grief to see]
> By wicked Hands shall Murdered be.

This, of course, is Head playing up to his Royalist readers, as is plain from the unctuous note:

Spoken concerning the Execrable Murther of that Pious Prince King Charles the First, the most Renowned for Piety, Prudence and Patience, of all his contemporary Princes throughout the whole World, of whom when all is said that can be spoken, yet doth all come farr short of his deserved praises . . .

Thus the unscrupulous Richard Head, in a total of more than a hundred lines of rhymed snippets of English constitutional history, started a fashion for the fabrication of Mother Shipton's prophecies that was to reach its climax in Victorian times. And we can picture him, as Aubrey's cameo suggests, hastily dashing off this doggerel to complete his sensational account of Mother Shipton in order to earn some ready cash.

A plausible touch, as he draws to a conclusion (1684 edition), is to pretend to sound a note of caution about accepting the validity of the last few prophecies:

Whether Mother Shipton were certainly the Author of all the last Prophetick lines is hard to say, but for ought we can find she lived to an extraordinary Age, and tho' she was generally believed to be a Witch, yet Multitudes that either read or heard her prophecies have had a great Esteem for them, and her memory to this day is much Honoured by those of her own Country.

He then rounds off abruptly, simply saying that a memorial stone was erected in memory of Mother Shipton 'near Clifton, about a Mile from the City of York, from which the following is taken':

> Here lyes she who never ly'd
> Whose skill often has been try'd
> Her Prophecies shall still survive,
> And ever keep her name alive.

I was amused to note, in a later edition, that the first line had been prudently changed to 'Here lies she who *seldom* lied'!

Is the whole of Head's chapbook, in fact, a tissue of lies? Well, although we cannot rule out the possibility that he included certain genuine traditions concerning Mother Shipton – including this first mention of her being born in Knaresborough – we can have little confidence in what such a rogue of a hoaxter tells us . . . And how gratified he would have been, this Rabelaisian humorist so well versed in the art of wheedling and deception, to see how over the years his fiction has been solemnly copied and quoted, spread over the internet and fed to the gullible world as though it were substantial biographical truth.

5

The Mystery of Mother Shipton's Birthplace

Where was Mother Shipton born? To ask this, of course, is to assume that Mother Shipton was a real person. The classic reference book, E.C.Brewer's *Dictionary of Phrase and Fable*, in its early editions went so far as to dismiss this 'so-called prophetess', saying that, as in the case of 'Mrs. Harris' in *Martin Chuzzlewit*, the imaginary crony of the Dickens character, Sarah Gamp, 'there's no sich a person'. And I know a professor of history who takes the same view, believing her to be entirely mythical. Yet it remains possible that there is a historical human being to be discovered at the beginning of any mythological process – or, as I prefer to describe it, the evolution of a legend, because I distinguish between *myth*, something imagined, and *legend*, which has a basis in history.

An obvious example is Robin Hood. He has been confused, fictionalised and sentimentalised, especially in films and television. But few would doubt that there was an actual person as the starting-point of the legend and fiction. There is, in fact, a parallel between Robin Hood and Mother Shipton in that different areas can claim to have had a long connection with the original person. Though Robin is habitually linked with Sherwood Forest, near Nottingham, traditions or place-names associated with him are found over a wide area – Barnsdale Forest (between Wakefield and Doncaster), Rothwell, Loxley, Hathersage, Halifax, Fountains Abbey, York, Catterick, Richmond, Robin Hood's Bay, Kirklees (where he is said to have died) and a dozen other places.

Mother Shipton appears to have got around even more than Robin Hood. According to Mackay's *Memoirs of Extraordinary Popular Delusions* (1852) she was said to have been born in Buckinghamshire, in the village of Winslow-cum-Shipton, and Mackay even reproduces an engraving of the thatched cottage reputed to be her birthplace. She was also believed to have been born in London, and *Blackwood's Magazine* asserted that she lived by the Thames in a small house 'on the Wapping Shore', the ruins of which were still to be seen (December, 1846).

Mother Shipton's House
Winslow-cum-Shipton, near Buckingham
from Mackay's
Memoirs of Extraordinary Popular Delusions, 1852

In the eighteenth century Mother Shipton was shown in effigy in various London museums, and portraits of her formed the 'sign of Mother Shipton' for several London inns. One of these, in Camden Town, survived until about 1990, when its name was changed to 'The Fiddler's Elbow', though it is still popularly known as 'The Mother Redcap', recently renamed 'The World's End' – a phrase associated with Mother Shipton. Mother Redcap bears a marked resemblance to our prophetess. Said to have been an ale-wife at the time of Henry VIII, she was a 'wondrously wrinkled', monstrously ugly woman who practised witchcraft and fortune-telling. Also known as 'Mother Damnable', 'Mother Huff' and the 'Shrew of Kentish Town', this Mother Redcap could easily have been confused with Mother Shipton, and may well have contributed to the grotesque and diabolical figure depicted by Richard Head.

Several parts of the West Country have associations with Mother Shipton. It used to be claimed that she was born in Somerset, near Orchard Wyndham Manor (Williton), where her tomb could be seen. From this area comes her prophecy, described to me by a local when I recently visited Watchet as 'just an old yarn':

> Watchet and Doniford both shall drown
> And Williton become the seaport town.

This was related to the fear of coastal erosion or inundation by tidal waves, as was another Somerset prophecy attributed to Mother Shipton, namely, that the spire of the St. Dubricius Church in Porlock would become a mooring-point for sea-going ships.

At the other side of the country, in Norfolk, traditions concerning Mother Shipton were so strong that it was sometimes claimed that she had been born there – and I have even seen an internet site with the statement that she was 'born in Norfolk, near Knaresborough'. In Norfolk also we find her predictions relating to changes in the coastline:

> The town of Yarmouth shall become a nettle-bush.
> Bridges shall be pulled up and small vessels sail to
> Irstead and Barton Broads . . . Blessed are they that live
> near Potter Heigham, and double blessed they that live in it.

Mother Shipton was credited with other Norfolk predictions. Some were local, such as the forecast that 'Chischick Church should be a barn, And Bromholm Priory a farm', and that after a fierce battle fought at Rockheath-stone Hill on the Norwich Road the blood would be so clotted it would be carried away by ravens! Other predictions were more general, such as that the summers would become so cold they would be distinguished from winter only by the leaves on the trees.

A little to the west, in Cambridgeshire, there was a tradition surviving into Victorian times of washerwomen celebrating 'Mother Shipton's Holiday'. On the Wednesday of Whitsun week they held tea-parties in honour of their patroness, and drank to Mother Shipton with tea laced with rum. An inn at Downham Market named 'The Mother Shipton' testified to her popularity over much of East Anglia, and there is still a Mother Shipton Inn at Portsmouth. This inn owes its name to the fact that the land on which it was built was bought in 1881 – a significant Shipton date, especially so near to Brighton, as we shall see.

In Oxford-shire, on the border with Warwickshire, it was believed that Mother Shipton was the witch associated with the Rollright Stones, situated just to the north of Chipping Norton. Further north, to the west of Birmingham, in the caves at Kinver Edge, there was on display (until the 1940s) an exhibit known as 'Mother Shipton's Chair'.

Mother Shipton was sufficiently well-known in Scotland for a fanciful version of her life there to be published in the late eighteenth century. Taking a leaf out of Head's introduction, Henry Lemoine claimed he had learned about Mother Shipton's move to Scotland from 'an Ancient Caledonian Chronicle in the Scottish dialect' and from documents found in Melrose Abbey. The husband of the prophetess, Toby Shipton, had a great estate near the site of Bannockburn, he claimed, where he moved with his wife and their daughter Peggy.

Mother Shipton seems to have been even better known in Wales, so much so, in fact, that in an early edition of Webster's *Biographical Dictionary* we read the surprising statement that 'Mother Shipton was the nickname of a Welshwoman'. Though I have failed to find any confirmation of a Welsh origin for Mother Shipton, the idea seems to have been supported by E.C.Brewer. He does not localise Mother Shipton in his *Dictionary of Phrase and Fable*, but in his posthumous *Reader's Handbook* (1925) he gives the additional information that she was 'T.Evan Price, of South Wales, a prophetess, whose predictions (generally in rhymes) were at one time in everybody's mouth in South Wales, especially in Glamorganshire'!

The widespread appropriation of Mother Shipton, with people assuming that she was born or at least lived for a time in their own locality, can be explained by a combination of her popularity and the absence of any definite statement about her birthplace in the earliest pamphlets. As we have seen, the latter undoubtedly give her a Yorkshire setting, more particularly in York itself, but she is also presented as a mysterious, larger-than-life figure, an ideal basis for legend. The position was admirably summed up in 1849 by the Reverend John Gunn, who wrote of Mother Shipton, when quoting her Norfolk sayings:

Yorkshire is reputed to have been her native county, but there is scarcely a place in which her vaticinations are not known; and, given they have reference to the immediate locality in which they are current, Mother Shipton, if indeed she had a real existence, must have been gifted with ubiquity and superhuman powers of locomotion; or else she may be considered 'a very Hercules of sayings', for her name has served as a hook to hang them on, just as that demi-god formed a nucleus for the collection of marvellous exploits.

The Yorkshire origin of Mother Shipton is supported by folklore which has no apparent connection with the early pamphlets we have considered. Writing in 1881, the Harrogate historian William Grainge mentioned several Shipton prophecies still maintained by oral tradition in Yorkshire. For example, she was supposed to have made predictions concerning Pickhill, in the North Riding, Ulleskelf, near Cawood, Northallerton, where the mound of Castle Hill would be 'filled with blood' and Walkingham Hill, three miles north of Knaresborough, which would 'run with blood'. Though there is no prophecy concerning Knaresborough in the early pamphlets, Grainge recorded one in local dialect which ran:

> When lords and ladies stinking water soss,
> High brigs o' stean the Nid sal cross,
> An' a toon be built on Harrogate Moss.

As *soss* (drink), *brigs* (bridges), *stean* (stone) and *toon* (town) are authentic local dialect this looks genuine, but Grainge believed it was no more than thirty years old, composed long after the development of Harrogate as a spa and later than the construction of the railway viaducts across the Nidd – one in Knaresborough and one nearby at Bilton. There are several other oral traditions like this, including one I recently came across to the effect that the prophetess

65

had forecast the expansion of Otley, on the Wharfe, saying it would reach from Clifton to the Chevin.

The claim that Mother Shipton was born in Knaresborough was first made, as we have seen, in 1667 by Richard Head. His chapbook was followed twenty years later by a shorter anonymous account, based on Head, but with a few items of additional information. This was *The Strange and Wonderful History of Mother Shipton*, published in London in 1686 for 'W.H.', presumably William Harris, for whom the 1687 edition of Head was printed. It was sold 'by J.Conyers in Fetter Lane', so we can conveniently refer to it as the Conyers Pamphlet. It opens with an interesting allusion to contemporary controversy about Mother Shipton's birthplace, and then Head's wording is copied, including his peculiar spelling of Knaresborough:

Mother Shipton [as all Histories agree] was a Yorkshire woman; but the particular place is very much disputed, because several Towns have pretended to the honour of her Birth; but the most credible and received opinion ascribes it to Naseborough, near the Dropping well in the County aforesaid;

This is followed by a brief summary of Head's story of the diabolical origin of the prophetess, who 'never had any Father of humane Race, or mortal Wight, but was begot (as the great Welch Prophet Merlin was of old) by the Phantasm of Appollo, or some wanton Airial Daemon'. Though much of Head's narrative is left out, Conyers has additions, such as the statement that when the Devil paid his daily visits to Agatha he made sure she was never short of money, and she would find, as she swept the house, coins such as 'Ninepences, Quarters of thirteen pence, half-pennies and the like'.

In this version, when Agatha is brought before the magistrate she points out two of his servant girls made pregnant by him. The strange noises which, according to Head, accompanied Mother Shipton's birth, have become in this pamphlet 'a most terrible clap of Thunder'. The date of the birth is given as 'in the Month of July 1488' – later than in Head, who implied that Agatha became pregnant in 1486. After the birth Agatha goes to spend the remainder of her days 'in the famous Convent of the order of St. Bridget, near Nottingham, in prayers and tears and other Acts of Pennance, to expiate the wickedness of her youth'. No record of such a convent,

66

incidentally, is known to historians. There are other variations, too. It is not the cradle that is suspended in the chimney, but the baby, 'stark naked, sitting a straddle upon the Iron to which the Pot-hooks was fastened'. And there is an anecdote telling how Mother Shipton made a woman thief declare at the market cross:

> I stole my Neighbour's Smock and Coat
> I am a Theif, and here I show't.

The Conyers Pamphlet also makes a point of correcting Head, who had consistently referred to the mother of the prophetess as Agatha Shipton. Her mother's name 'and consequently her Maiden surname', it states, was 'Soothtell' – patently an invented name, suggestive of 'soothsayer'. The first name of the prophetess, it adds, was Ursula, and she was baptised in this name on the orders of 'the Abbot of Beverly'. Ursula may well have been chosen by the writer as a name that seemed suitable for a prophetic witch. Though St. Ursula was the patron saint of educational institutes, a number of witches had this name – Ursula Flavin, for example, tried for witchcraft in Germany in 1581 and 1583, and Ursula Kemp, hanged at Chelmsford in 1582.

The Conyers Pamphlet, just like Head, makes no mention of Knaresborough other than in the opening reference. It does, however, unlike Head, suggest an explanation of why Mother Shipton became associated with York. In spite of her exceptional ugliness, we are told, at the age of twenty-four she married 'Toby Shipton, by trade a carpenter'. The writer does not say that Toby lived in York, or that the couple moved there, but this was always the assumption made in later pamphlets and chapbooks, mainly because much of the prophesying and Mother Shipton's death are set in York.

Here, with this mention of Toby Shipton, we have something like historical ground. Shipton (Anglo-Saxon 'sheep-enclosure') is common enough as a village name, and such places as Shipton-under-Wychwood in Oxfordshire have been associated with Mother Shipton because of the coincidence of name. This is why even the Yorkshire village of Shiptonthorpe, near Market Weighton, has been advanced as her birthplace. But the strongest claimant is un-doubtedly the Shipton four miles north of York, and this carpenter called Toby, named after his native village, seems entirely credible.

Documentary confirmation of his existence would be too much to expect, but I was delighted to discover, in the records of York Minster, evidence of a carpenter called Shipton, who worked on the fabric of the minster (1478-79), supplying ready-sawn planking. Payment was made to him as follows, for 104 planks of wood:

Laurencio Shipton de Tollerton pro ciiij tabulis serratis 7.2d.

This Laurence Shipton was a local man, Tollerton being the next village north of Shipton, and as he was active at the above dates I venture to suggest that in him we may have an ancestor of Toby Shipton – and even Mother Shipton's father-in-law!

The existence of an actual person called Mother Shipton becomes more feasible if we accept that Toby Shipton is not an invention, but a man who lived in York in the early years of the sixteenth century. If the Conyers figures are correct, the prophetess would have married him in about 1512, and this would give ample time for her to become established in York before Wolsey's intended visit in 1530. The very least we can say, if she existed at all, is that we must dismiss Head's silly supposition that she took the name of Shipton from her mother. That this was her married name is clear from our earliest source, the 1641 Lownds Pamphlet, which supports the Toby Shipton statement by referring to the prophetess – in the last lines – as 'Shipton's wife'. The first known foreign translation of the prophecies, incidentally, which is in Dutch (1667), states they are '*van Schiptons Vrouw*' (by Shipton's wife).

Now a York carpenter is more likely to have married a local girl than one who lived in a town about sixteen miles away – and the idea that Toby Shipton came specially to Knaresborough to woo a girl of repellent ugliness is by no means convincing. Yet Head says that her mother lived in Knaresborough, and that Mother Shipton was born in the same town, with the implication that the birthplace was near the Dropping Well.

In spite of Head's reticence concerning the Dropping Well itself, it may be that the mysterious and magical waters of petrifaction, which cover and infuse porous objects with a calcareous, stone-like deposit, gave him the idea that Knaresborough would be a most appropriate setting for the birth of a witch. From the Greek legends of Medusa and the gorgons onwards there had always been folklore associating witches with the power to petrify. The alternative explanation is that Head picked up some oral tradition of the town being her birthplace, and a later move to York, following her marriage, would in no way invalidate this.

The difficulty is that no other early writer appears to have known about the Shipton association with Knaresborough. What is particularly striking is that it is not even mentioned by John Leland, a kind of official historian and topographer appointed by Henry VIII. He came to Knaresborough in about 1538, only a few years after the Wolsey affair, when Mother Shipton would have been at the height of her fame. As her prediction of Wolsey's downfall could hardly have displeased the King, locals would not have hesitated to tell Leland of the Knaresborough connection – if it existed. In his *Itinerary* he gives a description of the town, the market, and Castle, and especially the Dropping Well, with which he is greatly impressed:

. . . a welle of a wonderful nature callid Droping Well, for out of great rokkes by it distillith water continually into it. The water ys of such a nature . . . that what thing so ever ys caste in, or growith about the rokke and ys touchid of this water growith ynto stone.

Yet Leland says nothing about Mother Shipton, who was eventually to become almost synonymous with the magic well. As the Knaresborough historian William Wheater (1907) remarked, 'the Antiquary's mission was to note all things noteworthy . . . Leland's silence as to Mother Shipton is fatal to her claims'. So is the silence of others, including the poet Michael Drayton, who in about 1612 described in verse both the Nidd and the Dropping Well 'which in a little space converteth Wood to Stone', but made no mention of Mother Shipton.

The most detailed description of Knaresborough from the early seventeenth century is in *Spadacrene Anglica, or the English Spaw Fountaine* (1626), a book written by Dr. Edmund Deane to publicise the town as the place to stay when taking the waters. He especially commends the chalybeate water of the Tewit Well on Harrogate Stray (the first to be called a 'spa' after the town in Belgium), also the water of the Old Sulphur Well or 'stinking spaw' in Low Harrogate and gives a full account of the famous Dropping Well:

The Dropping Well
from an engraving of 1746, showing cavities but no cave.

... the water whereof trickleth downe from the hanging Rocke over it ... falling in many pretty little streames ... divers inhabitants thereabouts say, and affirme, that it hath been found to bee very effectual in staying any flux of the body, which thing I easily beleeve.

Deane therefore recommeded these petrifying waters for internal as well as external use (no doubt useful as an antidote to the drastic purges caused by the Harrogate sulphur water!). But in this careful description of the Dropping Well and the town itself he gives no confirmation of Mother Shipton. Nor can I find any reference to her in diaries and letters of those who mention 'the Knaresborough Spaw', such as John Evelyn (1654), John Ray (1661) or Oliver Heywood (1666). And there is a touch of irony in the fact that William Lilly, in his own edition of Mother Shipton (1645), interprets the prophecy about 'Knavesmore' as referring to 'Knaresborough, by which the River Nidd runs'. But he says nothing about Mother Shipton being connected with this town, a point he would surely have made the most of.

This failure to mention Knaresborough as the birthplace does not rule out the possibility of some unrecorded oral tradition. Yet the remarkable fact is that, even after the publication of Head's pamphlet, nobody seems aware of a Shipton connection. The assiduous side-saddle traveller Celia Fiennes, for instance, who stayed in Knaresborough in 1697, gives her usual detailed account of local curiosities – but nothing about Mother Shipton. Another famous traveller was Daniel Defoe, who stayed in Knaresborough in 1717, when he visited the infant spa of Harrogate. He saw the Dropping Well, and chatted to his Knaresborough landlord, but was not apparently told anything about the prophetess whose sign he had seen in London.

Nor does the town seem to have made much of her as the century progressed. In 1792 the well was visited by Viscount Torrington (nephew of Admiral Byng), whose diary gives all kinds of details of the petrificatiions and Knaresborough society, but, once again, there is nothing about the prophetess.

The earliest post-Head reference I can find to Mother Shipton being born in Knaresborough is in the seventh and expanded edition of *A Tour through the Whole Island of Great Britain* (1769), originally started by Defoe, but revised by Richardson and others.

71

Liz Sayers (joint owner) with the author at the Dropping Well.
Far right is Mother Shipton's Cave.

After a description of the Dropping Well it simply says: 'Tradition tells us that near this Rock the famous Mother Shipton was born'. This phrase is copied in Hargrove's first edition of his *History of the Castle Town and Forest of Knaresborough* (1775), where it follows his careful description of the water trickling from the rock 'with a musical kind of tinkling', the suspended objects being 'encrusted or petrified'. This statement is repeated in the subsequent editions of Hargrove until well into the nineteenth century, but without any reference to a cave. It shows that towards the end of the eighteenth century locals certainly believed that Mother Shipton had been born in Knaresborough 'near this rock'. But how near?

The nearest habitation to the Dropping Well is at the other end of the beech avenue planted by the Slingsby family as a spa walk in about 1739, where it emerges at Low Bridge. If we are looking for the 'house' where Head claims Agatha gave birth to the prophetess, it would have to be somewhere here. So it comes as no surprise to find this location given in the diary of the traveller Charles

Fothergill, who visited Knaresborogh on the 17th August 1805. Here is part of his entry for that day:

I went to the Dropping Well to enquire about the time requisite to petrify certain substances. Birds' nests are encrusted in 3 months. I saw a Jackdaw that was petrified in one year, wigs which also required a year, a man's hat a year and a half . . . the rock itself is most beautifully tinted, and overgrown with beautiful moss and plants . . . As Mother Shipton was born so near it as the bridge, there is no doubt that the vulgar of the day believed there was some connection between her and the wonderful power of the water: in rude eyes, and when all this country was a forest, this well must have had a strange superstitious effect on the mind of the inhabitants.

This is plain evidence that, at the beginning of the nineteenth century, Mother Shipton's birthplace was reputed to be near Low Bridge. Also of interest is this early comment on the way superstitious people would have made a link between a reputed witch and the petrifying water.

Low Bridge, Knaresborough
with the seventeenth-century Mother Shipton Inn
at the entrance to the Dropping Well.

It is a pity that Fothergill does not give us the exact location. Nor are we helped by the interesting reference made by Dr. Adam Hunter in his *The Waters of Harrogate and its Vicinity* (1807), to the home of Mother Shipton, 'the Joanna Southcote of her day'. He simply says that, on leaving the Dropping Well, the path 'leads the visitor to the house – a fit situation for such a personage'. This suggests one of the cottages near the exit from the Dropping Well estate, close to the attractive seventeenth-century inn – variously called 'The Dropping Well' and 'The Mother Shipton'. This seems to be confirmed by the famous connoisseur of spas, Dr. A.B.Granville. In his *Spas of England* (1841) he gives a detailed account of his stay in Harrogate, including a visit to Knaresborough, where he mentions the various attractions ideal for the diversion of the spa visitor. He suggests a visit to the Castle on 'the loftiest rock that hangs over the deeply-embosomed Nidd', St. Robert's Cave, and the House in the Rock. He describes the latter, set in the cliff overlooking Low Bridge, then adds:

Or, lastly, he [the visitor] might proceed to the house beneath the cliffs, which boasts of having been the birthplace of that celebrated character Mother Shipton, whose knowledge of futurity puzzled even the poor prelate of Beverley.

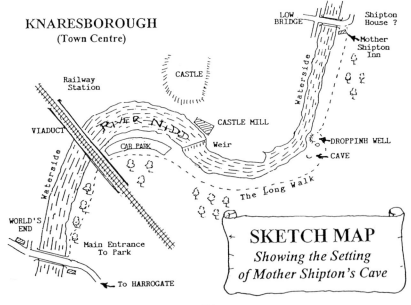

KNARESBOROUGH (Town Centre)

SKETCH MAP
*Showing the Setting
of Mother Shipton's Cave*

74

From this we can conclude that in Victorian times the birthplace of Mother Shipton was being shown to the public as a cottage near Low Bridge – probably one of those still remembered as the 'Shipton cottages', on a site just above the Mother Shipton Inn, where hollows in the magnesian limestone rock (originally for privvies and middins) seem to confirm Granville's location 'beneath the cliffs'.

A house reputed to be Mother Shipton's birthplace – presumably the same one – was still being shown to visitors until at least 1908, when it was seen by the distinguished author and authority on Yorkshire, J.S.Fletcher, who described it as being 'close by' the Mother Shipton Inn.

How, then, did the cave – just a few yards from the Dropping Well – come to be the new place of pilgrimage? There is no hint of a cave in any of the early Shipton literature, and for more than three centuries after the birth no visitor to the Dropping Well makes any mention of one. Most conclusive of all, none of the early engravings of the much-visited Dropping Well show a cave where one now exists. This is especially clear in an engraving made in 1746, where visitors are seen at a table and viewing platform, with a wall of rock behind them, containing fissures and cavities, but no actual cave.

Where did this mysterious cave come from? It is possible that for centuries it was obscured by vegetation. It is also possible that an opening appeared – or was greatly enlarged – after a rock fall. The magnesian limestone is easily eroded, and several falls or slippages of rock have been noted over the centuries. In 1704 the cliff-like mass which carries the dripping water suddenly moved towards the river, opening up a chasm three yards wide. Other significant changes were noted in 1816 and 1823.

Troglodites were not new to Knaresborough, an early example being the eccentric holy-man, Saint Robert (?1160-1218), who lived in a cave (still to be seen) about a mile down the river. The earliest mention I have been able to find of any kind of Shiptonian cave is in the early Victorian period. In about 1836 Dr. Doran of Knaresborough wrote a verse to illustrate a lithograph of the Dropping Well in which he spoke of the sorceress dwelling 'in yon cavern' – though as the picture showed the well itself as a kind of cavern, this is not conclusive. Defoe, in fact, had described the Dropping Well itself as 'in a little cave'. In 1845 a Knaresborough man exiled to Birmingham, John Watson, published a long poem about his boyhood in which he writes of Mother Shipton:

> Who in a cave liv'd near yon dropping well,
> And knew the power of every magic spell,
> In doggrell rhymes, wove in prophetic loom –
> A mystic web – chanting events to come . . .

A footnote to this gives a quotation from the *Aeneid* to show that Virgil had written of a cave inhabited by a witch and prophetess. Did this put the idea into Watson's head, or was he using it as a kind of confirmation?

> The mad prophetic Sibyl you shall find
> Dark in a cave, and on a rock inclin'd.

John Watson was perhaps the first to publicise a cave as the dwelling-place of Mother Shipton – but did he have a particular cave in mind? I was intrigued to come across a lengthy but obscure poem, published around this time, mid-century, by the Knaresborough farmer-poet, David Lewis, who lived at Belmont, not far from the Dropping Well. In this he includes a satirical account of Mother Shipton, in which he says that near the Dropping Well, skirted by the path through the wood, is a circular hole that was 'once a cave, now fallen in'. He imagines that this must have been where 'Nutty' (his name for the mother of the prophetess) was visited by the Devil:

> Nick, rambling out at evening hour
> Saw Nutty at the cavern door . . .

What is puzzling is that Lewis writes of a cave which had disappeared as a result of subsidence. One thing we can say for certain, however. By 1849 the Ordnance Survey map showed 'Mother Shipton's Cave', where it is today, presumably because this was what it was now being called by the locals.

Even so, in the course of the nineteenth century it is remarkable how little interest seems to have been taken in the supposed Shipton connection with the Dropping Well site. As in the two previous centuries, people continued to flock to the petrifying well for its own sake, not primarily because of any connection with the prophetess.

At the very beginning of the century, for example, the artist Joseph Farrington came to sketch the well, giving a full account of his visit in his diary (31 August 1801). But he did not mention Mother Shipton. John Nicholson, the 'Airedale poet' wrote of his admiration for the Long Walk in 1826:

> From the High Bridge to the fam'd tinkling well,
> With peace the coldest bosom here would swell . . .

He imagines the fairies that were supposed to dance in the area of the Dropping Well 'scorning old Mother Shipton's magic spell', but says nothing else about the prophetess. Certain gazeteers, such as the *Baines History, Directory and Gazeteer of the County of York* (1822) quote Hargrove's comment that Mother Shipton was born 'near this rock', but nineteenth-century guide books, whilst giving a full account of the petrifying well, say little or nothing about the Shipton association. The standard *Visitor's Handbook and Guide to Knaresborough*, published from 1850 to 1889, simply says that the prophetess 'resided near the Dropping Well'.

Mother Shipton's Cave
Liz Sayers (joint owner) and the author.

Disappointingly silent are interesting Victorian visitors, such as Frank Buckland, a surgeon in the Life Guards, who left a careful record of a visit to Knaresborough in 1863, especially to the Dropping Well, 'a massive frowning rock, over which a perpetual shower of water fell incessantly, with a musical and somewhat melancholy sound'. He noted that this was in the grounds of the Mother Shipton Inn, but said nothing about the prophetess herself – though he gave details of all the petrifactions, including a wig that had belonged to the Archbishop of York. I have in my possession a little booklet entitled *The Dropping Well of Knaresborough* (1881) written by a later distinguished visitor, the famous Baptist preacher, C.H.Spurgeon. In this he uses the analogy of petrifaction to describe the insidious effects of sin. Amidst the details he noted on his visit, however, there is no mention of Mother Shipton.

The influential *Jackson's Handbook for Tourists in Yorkshire* (1891) gives ample space to the Dropping Well, but dismisses Mother Shipton in a sentence. Other guides, like *Thorpe's New Illustrated Guide to Harrogate and District* (1891), offer her only as a tailpiece, an item of folklore not to be taken seriously. All that is said of her is:

Mother Shipton is generally supposed to have been born in this locality, but we have not observed that she occupies a place amongst the petrifactions.

This was the position during the opening years of the twentieth century. Local guide books, such as *Wood's ABC Visitor's Guide* (1901) now carried full-page adverts of the Dropping Well, remarkably, with no reference to Mother Shipton. There was, however, in the pages of the local guide book (from 1890), a mention of 'Mother Shipton's Cave':

the spot which has the reputation of being the place where Mother Shipton worked her charms, composed historical rhymes, told fortunes to credulous folk, invoked Satanic incantations, and generally exemplified the mysteries of witchcraft.

It adds that 'the entrance is uninviting', showing that the petrifying well, not the cave, was the essential place of pilgrimage.

So far there was no public claim that Mother Shipton had been born in this cave, merely that she had lived there. The reason was obvious. We know from the Fletcher reference that in 1908 the birthplace was still being shown as a house near Low Bridge – and he carefully distinguishes between this and the cave where she was supposed to have lived and 'whence emerged, timid or stimulated, the people who once flocked to hearken to her advice'.

Yet the tradition that the cave was where Mother Shipton was born had already been noted by the topographical author, Edmund Bogg, in about 1895 – and it was only a matter of time before the supposed dwelling-place became the supposed birthplace. The process was accelerated when J.W. Simpson took over as lessee, then proprietor, of the Dropping Well Estate. In particular, he shifted the emphasis from the well to Mother Shipton herself. From 1909 he began to advertise 'The Dropping Well and Mother Shipton's Cave', with the explanation, in minuscule letters under this title, 'The home of the Renowned Prophetess'. In his new guidebook on Mother Shipton (1910) he published a photograph of the cave – though without claiming it to be the birthplace. Whether he waited until the rival location at Low Bridge had ceased to be shown or whether he simply asserted that the cave was the true place, is not clear, but by the end of the First World War visitors were coming to Knaresborough to see not so much the Dropping Well as the cave, now actively publicised as Mother Shipton's birthplace.

It is easy to understand how Simpson and his successors were able to promote 'Old Mother Shipton's Cave', nowadays proclaimed to every passing car on the A1 and all approach roads to Knaresborough. The setting is perfect for the birth of a witch and prophetess . . . The music of the magical water dripping over the mossy brow of the rock, the river flowing past the Cave, the surrounding woodland with its air of mystery and antiquity . . . How understandable that the legend should have been taken to its logical conclusion and the birth declared to have been here!

Provided that this birthplace is described as 'legendary' or 'traditional', I can see no objection to its being imaginatively associated with Mother Shipton. As in the case of much-visited birthplaces all over the world, there is no reason why matter-of-fact historians should not relax a little, use their imaginations, and make a romantic suspension of disbelief.

6

The Changing Face of Mother Shipton

In this chapter we shall examine the iconography of Mother Shipton and at the same time take account of the variety of ways in which she has been presented to the public over the centuries.

The first known picture of Mother Shipton on the title-page of the 1641 Lownds Pamphlet, is a roughly-drawn woodcut which shows a woman in normal Tudor dress. The face, though not especially attractive, has none of the witch-like features which later became so familiar. However, as the text contained the implied accusation of witchcraft by Wolsey it is not surprising that illustrators of subsequent editions all exploited this by showing a hideous old crone, long before Head's horrific portrait in words.

There can be no doubt that, from the beginning, Mother Shipton was seen, not simply as a prophetess, but as a witch. This is implied by the very title of 'Mother' as we can deduce from the names of women referred to in witchcraft trials, such as those chronicled by C.L'Estrange Ewen. For example: Mother Waterhouse (1566), Mother Osborne (1579), Mother Pechey (1581), Mother Gabley (1583), Mother Bungie (1584), Mother Atkins (1592) and many more. Prophetic utterance was popularly associated with witchcraft, as we see in Shakespeare's *Macbeth* (1606). Witches were a familiar feature of society in the sixteenth and seventeenth centuries and even King James, who founded a school in Knaresborough in 1616, had made very plain his own opposition to witchcraft in his book *Daemonologie* (1597). In Knaresborough itself there is the well-documented case of a local schoolmaster, John Steward, tried for witchcraft at an ecclesiastical court in York in 1510. He was accused of keeping three bumblebees under a stone and calling them forth, one by one, to feed them with 'a drop of blode of his fyngor'. Moreover, he had used holy water to baptise a cock, a cat and other creatures. (No wonder Knaresborough Parish Church has such a ponderous font-cover!)

Whereas the Lownds 1641 Pamphlet had been illustrated by a nondescript Tudor woman, the first pamphlets to show Mother

Shipton as a witch appeared in 1642, when publishers added a dramatic touch to their reprints by depicting a confrontation with Wolsey. The finest of these appears on the title-page of *Foure Severall Strange Prophesies* (1642), printed in London for R. Harper. This is an extremely scarce pamphlet which adds to the Shipton prophecies others attributed to Ignatius, Sybilla and Merlin. It is plainly a Royalist production, referring to Charles I, 'whom God long preserve and protect from wicked plots of his enemies'. The illustration shows Wolsey on the left looking out from the tower of Cawood Castle, with Mother Shipton in the foreground. [See following page].

The features are severe and masculine, the eyes, nose and lips larger than normal, and there is a wart on the cheek. Yet this portrait has a certain dignity, and an awesome supernatural insight is well conveyed. If I had to choose one portrait of Mother Shipton, this would be it.

What is of particular interest about this 1642 pamphlet is that it describes the 1641 material as the 'Second Prophesie of Mother Shipton' and gives as the First a few lines of cryptic verse beginning:

> If Eighty Eight be past, then thrive
> Thou mayst till thirtie foure or five ...

This seems like a backward glance at 1588, when the Spanish Armada was defeated, and there are similar veiled references to 'the E' (Queen Elizabeth), 'a Scot' (James I) and the Gunpowder Plot. One curious feature of this so-called 'First Prophesie' is that it contains the only early hint that Mother Shipton may have made astrological predictions:

> In July month of the same yeere
> Saturne conjoynes with Jupiter

The rather sphinx-like nature of the portrait perhaps reflects the compiler's view that Mother Shipton spoke in riddles:

These lines [I confess impartially] are very mysterious and withal they are involved in a stupendous obscuritie, these seem as enigmatical as the Sphinx his hidden Riddle ...

Woodcut showing Mother Shipton confronting Wolsey
with Henry VIII and his first two Queens below.
First published in 1648 and used in the 1662 F. Coles edition,
it is much cruder than the 1642 woodcut on which it is based.

It is a pity that R. Harper did not retain this restrained portrayal of Mother Shipton in his later compilation, *Fourteen strange Prophesies* (1648). Mother Shipton had her due place in this, as in the whole series of prophetic anthologies which were now in vogue, increasing in length in proportion to the demand for them – *Six Strange Prophesies* (1642), *Nine Notable Prophesies* (1644), *Twelve Strange Prophesies* (1648), to give just a few examples.

Harper's new edition in 1648 has a woodcut based on the earlier version, but the art is much cruder, and it depicts Mother Shipton as a witch of repulsive ugliness. In addition to having the wart of the earlier Harper portrait she is now hideous with deep and extensive wrinkles. Her enormous hooked nose almost touches her prominent chin, and her narrowed eyes seem to glint malevolently in the direction of Wolsey on Cawood Tower. Her right hand is raised in a gesture of prophetic admonition, her left hand holds a symbolic staff of prophecy, and she wears a pointed cap. Her humpbacked figure helps to emphasise her extreme age – though if she was born in 1488, at the time of the Wolsey incident she would only have been 42!

This portrait of Mother Shipton certainly helped to strengthen and disseminate the idea that she was a witch. It also contributed to the classic idea of what a witch looked like. She was, after all, the only named witch whose features were familiar to the public. In addition, her marked resemblance to Punch raises the question of which of the two came first, and it is possible, as W.H. Harrison argued in 1881, that the puppet was influenced by the popular image of Mother Shipton. Harrison noted several features in common, especially the hooked nose and upturned chin, the cap and the humped back. He might have added that the name of Punch's dog, Toby, though traditionally derived from a Tobias of biblical times, happens to be the name of Mother Shipton's husband.

Whether connected with Punch or not, in the early eighteenth century Mother Shipton became a puppet in her own right, famous for her ability to smoke a real pipe during her performances. I was fascinated to discover that in the Musée de la Marionnette, Vieux Lyon, they not only have a puppet of Mother Shipton, but state that it is the *oldest known English puppet*, dating from the early eighteenth century. The wooden head of this marionette has two holes – one to hold the pipe, the other to release clouds of smoke. [See following page]. There is a similar puppet head of a pipe-smoking Mother Shipton in the Theatre Museum in London. In 1831 a report on Bartholomew Fair describes the puppet of this 'Yorkshire hag who will light and smoke her pipe'. The following year she was performing in New York, and the great puppeteer, Clun Lewis, believed that the Mother Shipton character had enjoyed popularity for at least two hundred years.

The surviving puppet heads suggest gypsy features rather than the grotesque profiles of 1648 and 1662. For real ugliness we need to turn to the horror-story descriptions in Head's *Life and Death of Mother Shipton*. The woodcuts could hardly do justice to them – but an attempt was made.

Mother Shipton, displayed as the 'oldest known English puppet' (early 1700s)
in the Musée de la Marionnette, Vieux Lyon.
First worked by rods, then by strings, the puppet smoked
— and is shown smoking — a real pipe.
(Reconstruction by Peter Kearney based on a photograph by G. Kriloff).

His 1684 edition shows her mother, Agatha, appearing before the magistrate as a hideous old woman, pregnant by the Devil, and yet the 1667 and 1687 editions show her as an innocent young maid sitting by the river-side and being seduced by a smartly-dressed young man. Looking on is the adult Mother Shipton, almost bent double with extreme old age, her crooked nose and jagged chin almost meeting. [See page 50]. This warts-and-all portrait served to confirm the earlier image, and showed the witch holding an enlarged staff – and what seems to be the kerchief she threw in the fire (in the 1641 prophecy). In the background of this frontispiece we also see a few small figures apparently related to Head's story, such as horses riding through the air and women upside down.

On the last page of my 1687 edition is another picture of Mother Shipton, as ugly as before, but with her hands together, and kneeling, as though in prayer. This is apparently from her tombstone 'erected near Clifton', near York. As Head had been so vague about her death, the Conyers Pamphlet (1686) expanded on his final paragraph, interpreting the phrase 'extraordinary age' as 73, though a slightly later edition changed this to 59!

At last being threescore and thirteen years of Age, she found the time in the Black Book of Destiny approaching, wherein she must give a final Adieu to this World, which she fore-told to a day to divers people, and at the hour predicted, having taken solemn leave of her Friends, laid her self down on her Bed and dyed ...

'Mother Shipton's Tomb', Orchard Wyndham, Somerset
(Drawing from booklet by William George, 1879)

It is interesting to note here that she had at least this in common with Nostradamus – the alleged prediction of the hour of death. The Conyers Pamphlet has the crudest woodcuts of all, and these are mainly of interest because they show Mother Shipton consulting what seem to be books of astrology and show an almost geriatric figure which helped to foster the image of 'Old Mother Shipton'.

The location of and appearance of her memorial stone deserves its share of attention. The place given by Head – about a mile out of York, on the road to Clifton (and Shipton) – continued to be mentioned in numerous pamphlets and chapbooks. A version that went through several reprints, first published in 1740, stated that 'a Monument of Stone was erected to her Memory' and that on it was carved a woman on her knees in prayer, which could be 'seen to this day'. This was almost certainly the stone which in 1847 was enclosed in a small garden. Contemporary accounts, however, show it to have been the tombstone of a medieval knight, set up vertically. It is described in the official handbook of the York Museum (1841) where I saw it many years ago:

A mutilated effigy, 4ft. 6in. long, which during a long period was placed, with the lower half buried in the ground, at the end of the village of Clifton, near York, by the side of the turnpike road leading to Easingwold. It is too much defaced to show the slightest indication of the knight it was intended to represent. The figure used to be called 'Mother Shipton's Stone' from the tradition that she was burnt to death by its side.

Here is an interesting development in the mythology – the only known tradition that Mother Shipton really had been burnt as a witch – possibly a local variant of the Wolsey threat. Confirmation that the stone was to be seen in situ in the first decades of the nineteenth century is given by the York historian William Camidge, writing in 1898. He says it was the figure of a warrior in armour, originally in a recumbent position, and probably from the ruins of St. Mary's Abbey.

It is a remarkable thing that a parallel myth developed at the other end of the country, where tourists in the eighteenth and nineteenth centuries came to see 'Mother Shipton's Tomb', situated in a wood on a hill near the manor house of Orchard-Wyndham, near Williton, in Somerset, where it still survives. It consists of a stone 7ft. tall by 3½ft. wide, on which is carved what appears to be a woman's head and shoulders, with a kind of starry halo above. [See page 85]. Below is an inscription in abbreviated Latin, which, to the ignorant might suggest some ancient mystery, but which could be translated: 'To the gods of the shades . . . Julia Martina lived twelve years, three months, twenty-two days . . .' So we must conclude that, far from having any connection with Mother Shipton, this was the tombstone of a Roman girl – or, at least, a copy of such a stone. Originally brought south to set up as a kind of fashionable folly by the Wyndham family, it was stated by a writer in 1879 to be 'a sham antique of the last century' copied from an engraving of an actual tomb noted by Camden. Later that year there appeared in the West Somerset Free Press both a comical letter about the tomb in Somerset dialect and a satirical poem by 'Russet Brown' in which he described an imaginary interview with Mother Shipton who is sitting on her tomb:

> A weird and wicked-looking hag,
> With cheeks as flabby as a bag,
> The nose that stood out from the face,
> Protruberous, large and void of grace,
> Hooked downwards from the chin to meet,
> Which upwards turned its friend to greet . . .

Mother Shipton complains to the poet about those who have been arguing about her tomb, 'seeking an antiquarian prize'. When she insists that this really is her burial-place the poet replies:

> How can that be? I've always heard
> That doubtful honoured is conferred
> On Yorkshire county, and e'en you
> Can't lie at once in places two.

Infuriated by this the old hag protests that the recent education laws have abolished superstition and tradition among the local rustics, but before this time, she says:

> The stone which now is standing here
> Was venerated far and near

As Mother Shipton's resting place,
The thought was sacred, not a trace
Of doubt the country people had
From peasant swain to farmer's lad . . .

The poem concludes with the witch uttering updated prophecies of doom and provoking a supernatural thunderstorm, and the whole piece is convincing evidence that Mother Shipton was a real talking-point in Somerset in the second half of the nineteenth century.

THE FAMOUS MOTHER SHIPTON

Mother Shipton with a scroll of her prophecies (1797)

Long before this discussion of the Orchard Wyndham tombstone it had been made clear that there was no genuine memorial to Mother Shipton, and in the early eighteenth century it is interesting to come across a serious proposal that one should be erected to her. This appeared in a letter published in *The Gentleman's Magazine*, (February 1736) written by an anonymous woman, one of the early feminists, who complains that though the magazine has done justice to women politicians, it has overlooked female supremacy in 'the Spirit of Prophecy':

The Oracles of the ancient Sibyls (who were all Women) have acquir'd such an established Reputation in the World that they will for ever do Honour to our Sex (especially) that celebrated Yorkshire Sibyl, Mrs. Ursula Shipton . . . and since Merlin, the Welsh Oracle, has had so much Honour done to him. I think It is a little hard that no notice should be taken of his Sister in the same Art.

As the writer goes on to give a summary of Head's account, apparently taking it at face value, we may wonder whether she is incredibly naïve, or simply writing tongue-in-cheek. Because of 'the great Character Mother Shipton hath so justly obtained by her predictions', she argues, she deserves a statue, and it is interesting to note that she would have her with a folklore wise-woman on one side and a real witch on the other:

I humbly propose it to the Ladies of Great Britain, who have the Honour of their sex and the Interest of Necromancy at Heart, that a magnificent Statue be erected to her Memory in some place of publick Resort, with Mother Bunch on one side as her Prime Minister and Mother Osborne as her Secretary on the other.

Nobody seems to have followed up the suggestion, no doubt because it was taken as ironical. The general view in the eighteenth century must have been that Mother Shipton was too ugly to merit representation. If we turn to *The Spectator* we can find evidence that she was proverbially hideous in a spirited essay on ugliness written by Richard Steele in 1710. In a bogus letter from 'Alexander Carbuncle' we hear of 'Old Nell Trot' who is adored by the 'President of the ugly Club' and who is so ugly that she is 'the very Counterpart of Mother Shipton'. A writer in another celebrated magazine, *The Tatler*, recalls a stone-cutter who claimed to 'improve' statues. 'I remember a Venus', he writes, 'that by the Nose he had given her, look'd like Mother Shipton'.

Drawing by Sir Ralph Ouseley of York (late 18th century)
showing a less hideous Mother Shipton
with an ape as a familiar

So familiar was the hooked nose of the Yorkshire witch that some time in the first half of the eighteenth century, or perhaps even earlier, a striking little moth whose forewings are marked with what looks like the profile of a long-nosed hag, was being called 'The Mother Shipton'. This was accepted as the standard popular name of the moth by pioneer entomologists such as Moses Harris in 1775, who also recorded its official name of *Euclidia Mi*.

Though Mother Shipton was a byword for ugliness there were always those who tried to show her in the most favourable light. Take, for example, the popular chapbook *Past, Present and to come,* or *The Renowned Mother Shipton's most surprizing Yorkshire Prophecies* (1740), printed for J.Tyrrel, which carries on the title-page a quotation from Dryden. The poet is presented as having lent his own considerable support to the claims of Mother Shipton by writing of her as follows:

> She, tho' from Heav'n remote, to Heav'n could move
> With strength of Mind, and tread th' Abyss above;
> And penetrate with her interior Light,
> Those upper Depths which Nature hid from Sight;
> And what she had observ'd and learn'd from thence,
> Lov'd in familiar Language to dispense.

This has frequently been copied or referred to as evidence that Dryden himself wrote of Mother Shipton. I recall being unable to find it after a long search through the poet's collected works – until I came across a section in his poem 'Pythagorean Philosophy', in which these same lines appeared. They have, in fact, nothing to do with prophecy, and are part of a section describing how Pythagoras advocated vegetarianism! By dishonestly changing 'he' to 'she' this 1740 editor or printer added another little lie to the Shipton mythology.

This edition even tries to outdo Head by claiming that it has been specially printed to reveal to the public a prophecy of Mother Shipton's 'which hath been preserved in Manuscript in Lord P--s's Family for several Ages', – a possible reference to a handwritten MS of 1620 associated with Lord Powis, in which I can detect no connection with Mother Shipton.

The importance of this 1740 *Past, Present and to Come* version, which was reprinted with variations well into the nineteenth century, was that it had the effect of upgrading the prophetess. For example, referring to Head's account of the monstrous birth it says that although the child was supposed to have been so 'warped and disturbed . . . the very Master-Piece of Deformity', nevertheless such reports were 'as full Romantick as the fabulous Intrigues of the Heathen Gods and Goddesses'. Mother Shipton was, this writer insists, not of devilish origin, but 'begotten by a man'. He dismisses most of Head's material by scorning to repeat 'Legends . . . so ridiculous and trifling' and the 'unaccountable and monstrous Stories and Fables'.

This means, of course, that he has little left to tell us, but at least he is able to improve on the 1686 name of 'Soothtell', saying that the child was baptised 'Ursula Sonthiel'. This is the name now most commonly seen, though over the years it has appeared as 'Southiel', 'Southeil', 'Southill', 'Sontibles', and even 'Southwick'. He also raises the status of Toby Shipton, describing him as a builder rather than a carpenter. Most of all, he speaks of exalting the prophetess to a level not seen in earlier writing:

'Tis assuredly and generally held, by most of the first Quality and best Judgement in the County of York, that she was a person of ordinary Education, but great Piety, and that she was supernaturally endowed with uncommon Penetration into future Things, for which she artfully became so famous in Time that great Numbers of all Ranks, Titles and Degrees resorted to her habitation to hear her wonderful Discoveries and Predictions.

Representations of her still showed witch-like characteristics, but she was now less horrific in appearance. An ivory carving, probably from the late eighteenth century, showed her with pointed cap, hooked nose and curved chin - but she was shown in the distingished company of other famous necromancers, including 'Friar Bacon and Dr. Faustus'. In 1797 a version of the prophecies printed in London for S. Baker carried a new portrait of Mother Shipton which had the familiar Punch-like profile, facing right, with a pointed, broad-brimmed hat, but she now held a scroll of prophecies. A little later there was published a picture 'in the possession of Ralph Ousely of York', unique in its inclusion of a monkey as a witch's familiar – yet the woman's face is that of a serious-looking prophetess, rather appealing in her melancholy.

On the other hand, many people saw Mother Shipton as a figure of fun, an image encouraged by the stage and pantomime versions we shall consider in the next chapter. In Mrs. Salmon's waxworks museum in Fleet Street there was an effigy of Mother Shipton with a mechanism enabling her to kick out at anyone who came too close, making her very popular with children. In Fleet Street, too, was Rackstraw's Museum, in which could be seen, according to the 1792 catalogue:

A figure of Mother Shipton, the prophetess, in which the lineaments of old age are strongly and naturally marked. Also her real skull, brought from her burial place at Knaresborough in Yorkshire.

This is of interest because, in addition to adding Knaresborough to the places where she is supposed to have been buried, it shows that Mother Shipton was being exhibited as a prophetess, not a witch. An 'exact figure' of her could also be seen in the 'curiosity house' at Stepney, and she even had her place amongst the wax effigies of kings and queens and other notables in Westminster Abbey. These were apparently carried at funerals and came to be known as 'The Play of the Dead Volks' and, later, when the costumes became tattered, 'the Ragged Regiment'. Mother Shipton could be seen in Westminster Abbey until 1839, when this macabre collection was dismantled.

Mother Shipton was now so well-known, and at the same time so indeterminate, that people could make of her what they pleased. One of the most striking examples of this is a political satire of 66 pages published by some anonymous MP in 1782, entitled *Saint Stephen's Tripod* or *Mother Shipton in the Lower H**se*. The rhymed 'prophecies' contained in this peculiar work are obscure and esoteric, full of allusions to individuals named only by initials, but it shows that Mother Shipton was so well-established as a folklore reference-point that she could be used for parliamentary humour.

A further example of satirical verse based on Mother Shipton could be found amongst the undergraduates at Cambridge in about 1821. During a debate on the Corn Laws a student named W.R.Praed, who later became MP for Great Yarmouth, made a famous maiden speech in which he quoted what he claimed was a prophecy of Mother Shipton, but which he had simply made up as he spoke. One of the verses recorded by a fellow-student ran as follows:

> When taxes for places and pensions
> Are levied without any qualms
> By a King of the purest intentions
> Who reads in the Prophets and Psalms ...

There was nothing new about putting words into the mouth of Mother Shipton, but a further twist in the business of filling the vacuum of her life-story with invented biographical details came with Henry Lemoine's account of her in *The New Wonderful Magazine* in 1793. The writer has no scruples in adding to a

93

condensed version of the earlier material all kinds of fictional touches. For example, when the child was born, he tells us, 'a raven croaked upon the chimneytop'. The prophetess was christened by the name of 'Janet Ursula Sontibles', and eventually became so famous that some of 'the quality' sent to ask for her advice from as far as 400 miles away, even from Wales and Scotland. According to Lemoine, when she was 'about thirty' she married Toby Shipton, 'a rich old carpenter', whose possession of 'a great estate' at Bannockburn enabled Lemoine to set his fiction in Scotland, saying that Mother Shipton moved there with Toby and her daughter Peggy, the latter wooed by a rich miller named Ralpho . . .

A few years later appeared one of the earliest of a whole series of chapbooks enlisting Mother Shipton as an authority for a collection of items on fortune-telling, the interpretation of dreams and so forth. Entitled *Mother Shipton's Legacy*, it was published in York in 1797 as an attractive miniature, measuring only 4 inches by 2½. There is no suggestion of witchcraft here, and much of it is addressed to children. It opens:

Halloo! Halloo! Halloo! What's the matter? Stand aside: here is old Mother Shipton! Now little boys and girls is the time to have your fortunes told by this wonderful old woman . . .

The picture of Mother Shipton accompanying this, notwithstanding a spider's web in the background, is of a normal-looking woman wearing a crinoline and bonnet. There are items for adults as well, such as details of lucky and unlucky days, the meaning of moles on the skin, magical tables in which a pin is to be stuck to predict the future, and especially the interpretation of dreams. Trivial though this little book may appear it was one which was treasured from childhood by the poet John Clare.

During the first half of the nineteenth century various booklets appeared claiming Mother Shipton as an interpreter of dreams. These really took over from earlier fortune-telling books such as *Mother Bunch's Closet*. We have, for example, *The Dreamer's Oracle*, 'being a Faithful Interpretation of Two Hundred Dreams by Mother Shipton'. This lists the commonest dreams, commenting on them in rhyme. Future trouble is seen, for example, in the symbolism of falling, losing teeth – and especially cats, to dream of which is always bad news.

Similar nonsense is given in *Mother Shipton's Universal Dreamer*, and *Mother Shipton's Fortune Telling Book*, the latter offering a 'sure Guide to Matrimony' and containing a thousand questions with a list of answers into which the reader stuck the customary pin, the whole claiming to be based on a newly-discovered old manuscript. Fortune-telling by cards and palmistry was included in the penny chapbook *Mother Shipton's Wheel of Fortune*, and her *Prophetic Almanack* whose title-page showed Ursula riding through the night sky on her broomstick. Similar material appeared in *The Gypsy's Oracle* 'by the celebrated Mother Shipton', published in London by J. Bysh, who also brought out a condensed 'Life' of the prophetess as *Mother Shipton, Queen of the Gypsies*.

Most of these printed fatuities were harmless, but Mother Shipton was also used as an authority for certain unsavoury folk remedies, such as the one noted by a Leeds surgeon in 1803. Visiting two children 'ill of the cough' (whooping cough) he discovered that the mother of this poor family was preparing to roast a brace of mice and get her children to eat them, because 'Mother Shipton's prophecies recommended this dainty dish as an infallible cure for the tiresome disease his medecines could not conquer'.

Another branch of the romantic exploitation of Mother Shipton is seen in several novelettes written around her. Typically late-Victorian both in illustration and general style is the twenty-one-chapter *Mother Shipton and her Prophecies: A Legendary Romance*. It tells the story of the dealings between the witch-prophetess and the fair Gresilda Branscombe of Eavenshell Hall, 'an old manorial pile which rears its antique and weather-beaten turrets on the outskirts of Knaresborough'. Gresilda, who is wooed by Sir Wrexley Clavering(!) is spoken to by Mother Shipton. Horrified that his beloved should be addressed by such a hag Clavering asks: 'Do you know her?' The reply given by Mother Shipton will serve to show the writer's style: 'Know her? Aye, by the rood, right well, I ween!' The illustrations show a severe, masculine Mother Shipton, reflecting the description in the text:

an old woman with an aquiline nose, deep dark piercing eyes, and a gaunt figure which appeared to be bent double under the weight of three score years . . . habited in a long red cloak, a quaint and curious mob cap decorated her head and she carried in her hand a crutch stick.

As recently as 1922 there appeared *The Witch of Knaresborough* a 'historical romance' by F. Rylstone Var. This contains a certain amount of local colour, with references to the topography and history of Knaresborough and district. Its story of how Ursula helps various good folk during the turmoil of the Wars of the Roses is not only anachronistic, but full of phoney dialogue. (Sample: 'Odd's bodkins and dirks!' quoth he). As by this time the cave was being actively promoted, the author brings it into the story by saying that the prophetess bought it after the death of her worthless husband Toby! The cover picture is of an attractive woman, more like a goddess than a witch, and is justified by description in the text:

She was small and slight, but held her proud, grey-tinged head so high that she seemed taller. Hers was the face of a deep thinker: that of a recluse and mystic . . . her eyes were keen frosty blue . . . her stern mouth could smile sweetly when she chose . . .

Dressed in a long blue robe, trimmed with silken embroidery and girded with a silver cord, from which hangs a 'silver-sheathed knife', Mother Shipton is now far removed from the harridan of the seventeenth-century woodcuts.

An aspect of the romantic treatment of Mother Shipton is the way she became the subject of verse, in particular, a strange narrative poem called *The Prophetess*, by Richard Brown, published in York and London in 1825. This purports to be a metrical version of the 'legend of Stockton Moor', set about three miles to the north-east of York. Possibly linked with the 'Stockmore' reference in the 1641 Pamphlet, this poem tells in obscure yet atmospheric language how a villager called Rob and his friends, supported by the priest, hang 'Mother Shipton, the witch of the moor'. The poet exaggerates, not the goddess-like prophetic features, but the wickedness of a sinister witch. So vile is this Mother Shipton that even as she hangs from the tree she mocks the attempt to kill her. The rope breaks, and they only succeed in hanging her when they strangle her with a withy – the flexible branch of a willow, deadly to witches:

Earth flinch'd, the trees shook, and all groan'd in despair . . .
And thus fell Mother Shipton of fam'd Stockton Moor!

In contrast to this versification of a grim legend is the light-hearted poem by David Lewis, previously referred to. In doggerel of considerable merit this Knaresborough farmer-turned-schoolmaster wittily satirises the Shipton myths. For example, using the dialect word 'mouldewarp' (mole) and a topical reference to the first tunnel under the Thames constructed by I.K. Brunel (1825-43), he writes:

Some witches often are at loss
When they have got a stream to cross
But she at will could make a tunnel,
Which gave the first idea to Brunel,
A Mouldewarp from shore to shore,
There never was so great a bore . . .

Yet for each writer who poked fun at Mother Shipton, and Lewis dismissing her as 'a great bore', there were others who took her seriously. A unique example of this is a handwritten pamphlet in the British Museum, donated by Sir William Strickland, who in 1914 wrote and illustrated a curious little poem inspired by a visit to the Dropping Well. Having set the scene, he writes:

Here a witch long ago dwelt alone;
Where the crag's dewy lip Turns its moss to stone
Yawned a cave. Far within it Rocking to and fro
Mother Shipton watched her kettle swing in the russet glow.
What herein, Stewed or brewed, Who can guess?
Tripe of Child, Hangman's gift for the Sorceress?
Hand of thief? Judge's ermine? All the nastiness
That by incantation can be made to curse or bless . . .

Sir William's own illustrations of his poem include Mother Shipton shown as a petrifying gorgon, with serpents for her hair and a dagger through her head emerging as a tongue. This is, however, a rare and eccentric view, the personal concept of a latter-day romantic, and was not intended for publication.

Some odd things have happened to Mother Shipton. This was the name of a prostitute thrown out of the American mining town of Poker Flat in a 1928 play based on a story by Bret Harte. And the most bizarre Shipton fantasy I have come across is a kind of traditional anecdote recorded by the BBC in 1955, related in dialect by an elderly man living in Barrow upon Humber:

'Ave you 'eard the 'istory of Mother Shipton's 'ouse blowin' away? It blew 99 miles yonside the moon. I went in search of it . . . Then I met old Jack the Coachman, who was drivin' two led 'osses and an empty carriage loaden wi' 8,000 million magpies who 'ad drunk tea while they was as black as a pass o' snow. He said: 'If you want to find Mother Shipton she's at the bottom o' the sea, makin' steel 'ats out o' deal boards . . .'

As far as the general public was concerned the tendency, especially since the end of the First World War, was to see Mother Shipton not so much as a fantasy figure but as a legendary prophetess. The best-known representation was in the popular booklet of her prophecies sold by William Parr, the Knaresborough printer, based on the old inn-sign, said to be '200 years old, painted on copper'. In this Mother Shipton is still depicted with a broom – but it is held as a walking-stick, and she stands quite erect, holding a wicker basket and wearing a bonnet, cloak, neat white apron and simple cloak. In the inn-sign her black cat gives a hint of sorcery, but in most versions it is omitted, and in spite of the narrow eyes and irregular features, this figure could be taken for an old lady on her way to Knaresborough market.

The presentation of Mother Shipton as an amiable prophetess is one favoured today, with the witchcraft element played down. So, although the seventeenth-century wood-cuts of a hideous, misshapen ogress had an immense influence, and were a principal contribution to the stereotype image of an English witch, the usual modern representation of Mother Shipton has come almost full circle and is more like the original wise-woman who illustrated the first pamphlet in 1641.

Mother Shipton was a wise woman and knew a good place. Come and try

Knaresborough

Late Victorian novelty postcard based on the old inn-sign. The figure opens up to reveal a neatly folded list of rhymed prophecies.

7

Mother Shipton on Stage: Pantomime Dame

A little-known facet of Mother Shipton is that for several generations she was known to the general public, not so much through pamphlets or chapbooks, but as an actual figure to be seen and heard in the English theatre. Indeed, I consider her to have been the very first pantomime dame, her role always being played by a man. She was also arguably the first fairy godmother, as we shall see – an ugly but kindly benefactress with supernatural powers.

The dramatic possibilities of Mother Shipton must have been apparent in the first edition of Richard Head's grotesque and colourful 'life' of 1667. The following year saw the publication of a quaint little pamphlet entitled *Mother Shipton's Christmas Carrols with her Merry Neighbours*, a copy of which survives in the Bodleian Library. That it derives from Head is proved by the woodcut facing the title-page – almost identical with the one illustrating Head's 1687 edition. A London publication, it was printed 'by P.Lillicrap for William Harris in Dunnings alley in Bishopsgate-street, 1668'.

The pamphlet, which contains blatant vulgarity absolutely characteristic of Head, purports to present certain exploits of Mother Shipton during the Christmas season, opening with a song and concluding with 'a witty Dialogue between Roast-Beef, Mince-Pye and Plumb-Pottage'. There is no record of this having been performed on stage, but it could certainly have been used for private performances, perhaps by carousing friends during Twelfth Night revels, and the verse on the title-page gives a hint of the jolly dame of Christmas pantomime:

> Here Mother Shipton doth her self present
> In pleasant Carrols for your merryment,
> 'Tis a strange case if she doth not appear
> Handsome enough with such good Christmas cheer,
> Roast-Beef, Mince-Pye, Plumb-Pottage, such sweet stuff –
> Prophesie choak her if she han't enough,
> Read o're the Title, and what follows after

'Twil fill your heart with joy, your tongue with laughter.

The opening song in celebration of Mother Shipton's phenomenal ugliness embroiders on the prose account of the earlier chapbook. Here are a few typical verses from the total dozen, almost certainly written by Head himself:

> Her Beetle Brows forget I not
>   nor teeth as white as Amber,
> Her Face did shine like pewter pot
>   belonging to the Chamber
>
> Her Saucer eyes of Cannon bore
>   were big ten times as thine,
> Like powdering Tubs still running o're
>   or full of standing brine
>
> But shall I speak as to her snout
>   the matter in't and fat on't
> Which like a Hunters Horn stood out
>   a man might hang his hat on't ...
>
> Her Breasts so tempting and so fair
>   like two old foot-balls look
> Which you might see through smock so rare
>   and black as the pot-hook.
>
> Her Waste was slender, but her Bum
>   rises so high you'd say
> Each Buttuck seem'd a Kettle drum
>   stuft with a Truss of Hay ...
>
> But for those parts which are unseen
>   I cannot well express;
> 'T would fright the Devil himself, I ween,
>   to see her nakedness.

Notwithstanding her repulsive physique, Mother Shipton 'having pick'd up a little money to be merry with at Christmas, she very lovingly invites half a dozen of her neighbours to partake of it.' Her neighbours are all 'good old women' who love tender food that needs no chewing, such as beef 'well boyled', as well as mince pie and Plumb-pottage' – the porridge-like forerunner of Christmas pudding.

Head – for in this passage, especially, we cannot doubt that he is the narrator – now describes how Mother Shipton takes revenge on her neighbours (apparently because they had failed to return her washing-tub and broom) by administering a magical substance: 'This Powder she infused into a Pitcher of good Yorkshire stingoe' (strong beer) into which the old women 'tippled their Noses most plenteously'. The effect of the potion – a favourite phenomenon with the scatological Head – was to make the women break wind uncontrollably:

one unawares let go such a Hummer as to set all the rest a twittering, that presently all of them in like manner began to discharge with such resolution as if they had been about battering a fort.

Mother Shipton seeing the efficacy of the Powder began to be so very pleasant, and told them they plaide their cards well sure by reason of their trumping about so roundly.

She then completes her revenge on her neighbours now 'bespattered' and 'shitten', by sending them out into the fresh air of the 'cold, frosty fields', at the same time creating the illusion that they are walking in deep water. The result is that they hold their skirts high above their heads and are the laughing-stock of the townsfolk who follow them 'shouting and throwing rotten Eggs and Apples at their arses all the way they went'.

These and several other trivial vulgarities allegedly caused by the hideous witch could hardly have been represented on a stage. The concluding Dialogue, however, could have been the basis of a pantomime-style entertainment. It features four characters – Roast-Beef, Mince-Pye, and Plum-Pottage 'contending for superiority', with a kind of referee in the person of Strong-Beer, 'their Moderator thereupon'. Having shared a drink together the characters open a debate on which is to be regarded the most important component of Christmas. Plumb-Pottage claims that he should be the first dish on the table, simply because of 'Ancient Custome'. Mince-Pye, however, retorts:

Pish! Never tell me of your Reasons: your Reasons are not in Date ... and as for Custome, I say 'tis more Customary to prefer Pye before Pottage.

Roast-Beef, however, pleads royal approbation:

I am Beef, a good substantial food, a dish for a Prince and indeed, as 'tis recorded, the King of meats ... And not without cause considering the Dignity his Royal Majesty King James was pleased to confer upon me, which one day coming down into his kitchen, I gave him such satisfaction that he daign'd me with the Honour of Knighthood, with the title of Sir Loyne, and hereafter claim precedency over these mincing Mimicks.

Plumb-Pottage objects that Beef is not a special Christmas favourite like himself, and Mince-Pye claims he gives festive delight particularly to the ladies as 'a dish full of dainty'. The verdict finally delivered by Strong-Beer is that each of the three has his rightful place at the Christmas table, and so has he, the point being driven home in the concluding drinking-song.

This curious little sketch seems artificially attached, and, being devoid of coarseness, was surely not contributed by Head. The piece as a whole, however, does have the effect of giving Mother Shipton a place amongst the Christmas revelries of post-Restoration England.

The aptly-named Peter Lillicrap may not have managed to get Head's vulgarities on stage with this slight and silly pamphlet, but it was he who published the first known dramatic version of Mother Shipton. This was a play with music entitled: *The Life of Mother Shipton, a New Comedy. As it was Acted Nineteen dayes together with great Applause.*

None of the extant copies carries a date, but internal evidence shows it to be post-Head. The author is given as 'T.T.', who can be identified as Thomas Thompson, an obscure Restoration playwright. Thompson had dramatised Head's *The English Rogue* in 1668. No doubt he turned to Head's *The Life and Death of Mother Shipton*, hoping it would provide him with material for another play. In this he must have been disappointed, finding little or no plot, and such bizarre fantasy that no straightforward dramatisation was possible.

What he did was take a minimum of Head's material and make the most of Shipton as a magical figure, who, though the offspring of the Devil, finally outwits him. Much of the play, in fact, is filled out by borrowings from Middleton's *A Chaste Maid in Cheapside* and Massinger's *A City Madam*, as we find in the early scenes where Mrs. Love is seduced by the character Shiftwell. The setting is partly in York, partly in 'Naseborough Grove in Yorkshire', the home of Mother Shipton, styled as 'Agatha Shipton, the daughter of Solomon Shipton, Ditch digger, lately deceased.' She makes an appearance in the sixth scene as someone who has already gained national notoriety:

Now both in mind and form I am a perfect Witch. What hitherto I have done has spread my fame far wider than it is, so that those who before looked upon me as a crack-brained woman, now begin to admire me and esteem my words as Oracles.

In spite of its title the play tells us almost nothing about the life of Mother Shipton, and gives little specific about the prophecies, but has the 'Abbot of Beverly' taking Mother Shipton before the magistrate and putting forward various yokels as witnesses to her having practised witchcraft. They are prevented from testifying by a devil in the guise of Radamon, who makes use of a simple device:

Greg: An't please your Worship I can safely take my corporal oath
       she is a — [Snezes]

Abbot: Out Rustick! are you not ashamed to sneze in the justices
        face?

Hod: An't please your Worship I dare take any oath too that she is
      a — [Snezes]

Abbot: More insolence like this will ruine me.

Jug and Bab: An't please your good Worship to take our oathes, and
             we will confidently swear that she is a — [Sneze]

Abbot: Devilish conspiracy! an oath sticks in each throat and none can gulp it out.

Justice: Pray, Sir, What was your meaning by these mechanicks here to deride me? [To Shipton] Are you guilty of what they accuse you of or no?

Shipton: No, right worshipful Sir, and here I do defie what all of them out of malice have most disgracefully termed me.

Justice: Once more speak you, or any, or all of you, can you contradict her, can you prove her a Witch?

Omnes: Yes an't please we can all swear she is a — [Sneze]

The magistrate sends all the sneezing witnesses to prison for contempt of court and for maligning Mother Shipton, 'a woman of good repute and conversation'. We now see Radamon reminding the prophetess that it is he who has saved her, but as the play proceeds she becomes impatient of her dependence on him and realises that she will ultimately pay for her supernatural powers in Hell. Her soliloquy is important as a turning point in the development of a benign, socially-acceptable Mother Shipton:

Now I am experienced in the Magical Sciences, as much as ever was the fam'd Medea or Circe, whose cunning has left a wonder to the world. So shall Shipton's too! but to what end? What will the applause and clamour of the world benefit me when endless torments are my only comfort?

So Thompson portrays Shipton as rejecting the demon who empowers her – but at the same time managing to retain her ability to prophesy. Pluto, the Devil in person, vows he will have her soul, but the powers of good soon prove superior. To the sound of 'soft Musick' an angel appears to succour the repentant prophetess:

Shipton despair not, but in hope grow strong,
Thou shalt find Mercy though thou hast done wrong.

The powers of evil do their worst, but all is in vain: 'The Devils poke with their rakes and cannot touch her'. Thompson here looks back to the mystery plays, and turns his comedy into a kind of religious tract:

Pluto: What preservative has she got against our power?

Radamon: Too sure she is shielded by those powers above against which ours
                are impotent!

The denouement comes when Mother Shipton snatches from Pluto a paper containing magic prophetic spells, but rejects all further contact with the kingdom of evil:

Shipton: Well, I accept your presents, but spurn your society, all your
                temptations are too airy and too weak to besiedge my fortyfied
                soul.

Pluto: Was ever Devil gull'd so?

        [Sings] Well lets descend and all Hell shall howl
               This full fortnight for losse of Shipton's soul!

(Exeunt with horrid Musick)

Shipton: So let them roare:

        [Sings] Wilst I do all their Hellish Acts despise
               The higher powers make me truly wise.

Thus Thompson presents the public with a converted Shipton whom he has transformed from malevolent witch into divinely-inspired prophetess. The importance of his play, however, was that it moved Mother Shipton further in the direction of pantomime, something we see particularly in her final speech, made directly to the audience, in the manner of a dame, and probably the basis of the Shipton monologue written in the following century by David Garrick:

        I've escap'd the Devil, but I fear you most:
        If your frowns appear poor Shipton's lost!

But now I look agen, me thinks I spy
A gentle pardon in each gratious eye.
Visit me oftner and in time you'll see
Poor Shipton may deserve your plaudite.

As Thompson's musical play was first performed by George
Jolly's troupe for nineteen successive days it must have had
considerable influence, helping to popularise Mother Shipton and
leading, perhaps, to a more serious treatment in the only known
opera to be based on her. This was *The Life of Mother Shipton and
the downfall of Cardinal Woolsey*, performed at Punch's Theatre and
announced as 'a new opera' in the *Daily Courant* of the 11th April,
1712. No composer is mentioned, and on further investigation this
turns out to have been a marionette show in Martin Powell's popular
string-puppet theatre in Covent Garden, repeated in subsequent
years, anachronistically smoking her pipe.

During the eighteenth century Mother Shipton become a popular
figure in Christmas pantomime. One of the people responsible for
this – and for an interesting reason – was none other than that most
versatile of actors, the great David Garrick (1717-1779). In 1747 he
had taken over as joint actor-manager of Drury Lane and felt he
needed to compete with the founder of pantomime, John Rich, at
Covent Garden. Garrick was not especially fond of pantomime but,
following Rich, he had played a lively Harlequin and, in 1759, he
collaborated with the manager-playwright, George Colman, to write
and produce *Harlequin's Invasion or a Christmas Gambol*. This was
a vital turning-point in the evolution of pantomime which until then
was literally mime, in so far as Harlequin was not a speaking part.
Now Garrick made him articulate for the very first time – and
moreover linked him with Mother Shipton.

For years I had been trying to find one of the monologues written
and performed by Garrick, which I had seen referred to as 'a trifling
entertainment', and described as 'Mother Shipton's Review of the
Audience'. Then, just before completing this book, I was delighted
to track it down (with timely help from the Theatre Museum) to the
archives of the museum in Hereford, Garrick's birthplace. The
manuscript carries no date, but the interesting thing is that it is
entitled: 'Prologue for Mother Shipton to a New Speaking
pantomime'. So it seems to me that this could well have been a

curtain-raiser for the ground-breaking 1759 pantomime, though it survived Garrick and was later used to introduce several other productions.

The manuscript opens with stage directions: 'Upon the drawing up of the Curtain – thunder and lightning – Mother Shipton rides across the stage on a broomstick – and then enters.' Garrick, who would have played this part himself, appears as an exuberant old witch, complaining about having to ride a hundred miles through the stormy sky, soaked to the skin . . .

> To wish you much joy – ere the Gambols begin,
> The joy of the Season (curtsies) for I hope, like your Sires,
> You love merry Christmas, good Cheer and large fires,
> Plumb porridge, minc'd Pyes, Capons, Spareribs & Turkies,
> For the Palate and Grinders how pleasant such work is!

He/she now takes the opportunity, as the mother of Harlequin, to deplore recent French cultural influence:

> Keep a bit of Old England, I beg and beseech you . . .
> Mother Shipton you see full of parent affection,
> For her only Son Harlequin prays your protection:
> Since I brought him before you, I've taught him to speak
> Not French parlez-vous, soft Italian or Greek,
> But true English Lingo and rigdum fun jokes
> Fit for rantipole Christmas, and Holiday folks!
> Laugh out my good friends, till your buttons all fly . . .

['Rigdum' was the name of a witty courtier in a play by Henry Carey; 'rantipole' refers to noisy romps.]

Garrick then puts on his spectacles so he can take a closer look at the audience, and in the manner of a modern stage comedian picks out and addresses individuals:

> What's the noise in that box (looks up) if Malice is in it
> I'll mount my swift Nag and whisk round in a minute;
> There's a face that looks glum – full of Mischief and Strife.
> (looks in Pit)

Oh, no, Sir – Your pardon – you sit by your wife –
Be but kind, my good friends, to my Son's Christmas Pranks,
I'll give you a prophecy mixed with my thanks . . .

After commenting on the ladies, with their fashionably huge
hair-styles, as well as other categories in the audience, including the
tongue-wagging gentlemen and the girls looking for husbands,
Mother Shipton praises the soldiers and sailors present, then rounds
off her little curtain-raiser with:

Be muzzled ye Criticks, that ye mayn't bark and bite,
And our happy Year will begin from this Night –
But I tarry too long – so I wish you Goodbye,
My Broom's ready saddled, and away I will fly.

The engraving described on the next page, satirising George Colman (1772),
author of the popular pantomime featuring Mother Shipton
as a benevolent supernatural dame. Colman is being pampered by her and fooling
about with Harlequin, who is trampling Shakespeare underfoot.
(Brotherton Collection)

109

Although this prologue is undated, from its title and its emphasis on Harlequin having been taught to speak proper English, it certainly looks as though it could have been used for the 'new speaking pantomime' of 1759, the text of which shows Harlequin (played by Thomas King) speaking fluent and witty English. Whatever the date, I find it quite exciting to think that in Garrick's little prologue we see Mother Shipton involved in the birth of the modern Christmas pantomime, and can claim her as the first real pantomime dame. We are accustomed to think of the pioneer dames of the nineteenth century and the women characters played by such men as Grimaldi and, later, Dan Leno. Yet Mother Shipton was well established as a female impersonation long before, and it could be argued that if Garrick had not used her to teach Harlequin to speak English, pantomime might long have remained the musical dumb-show that it was in other countries.

The success of Mother Shipton in Garrick's curtain-raiser seems to have led to her being used as a standard pantomime character, and a major success involving her was later achieved by his co-writer, George Colman. At the Theatre Royal, Covent Garden, he presented on the 16th December, 1770 *The New Pantomime Entertainment of Mother Shipton*, with music composed by Samuel Arnold. It ran, over two seasons, to 58 performances, and led to the playwright being satirised by an engraving which was captioned:

> View Colman in the Lap of Mother Shipton;
> A better Subject Satire never whipt on!

The plot involves Harlequin and Columbine, who are befriended by Mother Shipton. The action would have been brisk, full of elaborate stage tricks in the tradition founded by the enterprising John Rich.

Mother Shipton, played by a man, the popular actor-singer F.C.Reinhold, appears in Scene III, which is set in 'Mother Shipton's House'. Her recitative instantly informs the audience that she is a kind-hearted protectress rather than a forbidding witch:

> Thy Mistress lost! a Trifle; don't despair!
> Old Mother Shipton shall dispel thy Care;
> For thou shalt follow, and regain the Fair.

She then sings a song of particular interest in that it shows that in 1770 Mother Shipton still had a reputation for frightful ugliness, as well as for magical powers:

'Tis true I'm a Fright,
But a merry old Sprite,
And thou shalt be jovial, sweet Lad;
Full of Frolick and Glee,
Thou shalt revel like me,
Nor know what it is to be sad.

This magical Sword,
Ev'ry Bliss shall afford,
Wave but this, and enjoy without End!
From the deep, from the Air,
Ready Imps shall repair,
Elves and Goblins thy steps shall attend.

The scene changes from her house to the Dropping Well, something not mentioned in later versions of the pantomime.

This setting affords the opportunity for dancing by 'Goblins and Fairies' who display their 'Hoppings and Hobblings . . . Frisks and Vagaries.'

As in the later version, Harlequin is imprisoned in 'a Coal Pit'. Mother Shipton now promises Columbine her supernatural aid, singing:

Flash, ye Lightnings; rumble, Thunder:
To receive us, open, Earth!
Cease, my Daughter, cease to wonder!
Mother Shipton brings thee Mirth!

The two then sink into the ground amidst thunder and lightning.

The finale, Scene XXIV, takes place inside the Coal Pit, where Mother Shipton rescues Harlequin and unites him with Columbine. Her lines, once again, constitute an early example of what was to become the facile, rhymed couplet so universally typical of pantomime:

111

Hold, hold your desp'rate Hands! and know
'Tis Mother Shipton who forbids the Blow.
Safe, by your Side, your darling Daughter stands;
This is my Boy, and thus I join their Hands.
To work their Bliss, I'll ev'ry Art employ,
Hence Grief and Darkness; enter Light and Joy!

Arising from this pantomime, and probably also referring to later versions, was a song which long outlived all the stage productions, sung to the tune of 'Nancy Dawson' (i.e. 'Here we come gathering nuts in May'). Early collectors of ballads were often baffled by the content of this song, assuming that it could only be explained in terms of Shipton prophecies. But it is simply a popular song, in the real sense of the term, reflecting the success of the 1770 pantomime and the versions which followed it, with clear references to the spectacular stage effects, including the launching of a ship . . .

Of all the pretty pantomimes
That have been seen or sung in rhymes
Since famous Johnny Rich's times,
    There's none like Mother Shipton!

Near to the famous Dropping Well,
She first drew breath, as records tell,
And had good beer and ale to sell
    As ever tongue was tipt on;

Her Dropping Well itself is seen,
Quaint goblins hobble round their queen,
And little fairies tread the green,
    Called forth by Mother Shipton.

Oh, London is a charming place,
Yet grumble not ye critick race,
Tho' Mansion House is seen to grace
    The streets in Mother Shipton.

You think a blunder you decry,
Yet you might see with half an eye

112

'Tis Mother Shipton's prophecy,
Oh, charming Mother Shipton.

Come, jolly tars and sailors staunch,
Oh, come with us and see the launch,
'Twill feast your eyes, and fill your paunch,
As done by Mother Shipton.

The shores give way, the hulk that prop
Huzza! the ship is launched – and pop!
'Tis turned into a baker's shop,
Oh, charming Mother Shipton.

Then after several wonders past,
To Yorkshire all return at last,
And in a coal pit they are cast,
Oh, wondrous Mother Shipton.

Yet she redeems them every soul;
And here's the moral of the whole –
'Tis Mother Shipton brings the coal,
Oh, charming Mother Shipton.

The first two lines of the second verse were painted on the sign of the Mother Shipton Inn. Unaware that they were simply taken from a light-hearted popular song, the writers of local guide-books have tried to give them an air of mystery and authority they do not possess.

Mother Shipton became so popular in pantomime that she gained an accepted place alongside the usual stock characters of Harlequin, Columbine, Clown, Pantaloon etc., such as in a performance at Covent Garden on the 23rd February, 1778, when Mother Shipton was played and sung by 'Mr. Baker', probably the Thomas Baker who had appeared in Rich's pantomimes. Another piece had the odd title *Mother Shipton, her Wager, or Harlequin, Knight of Love and the Magic Whistle*. The performances were not confined to the Christmas period. For example, the pantomime *Mother Shipton or Harlequin Gladiator* was performed at Hammersmith on the 15th July, 1785. As usual, the part of Mother Shipton was played by a man, this time 'Mr. Wellman', whose wife played Columbine, and the show included several songs.

The most successful pantomime to feature Mother Shipton was undoubtedly the spectacular production *Harlequin's Museum or Mother Shipton Triumphant*, which was performed many times at Covent Garden between 1792 and 1794. Though the prophetess did not occupy the stage for anything like as long as Harlequin, her importance as a kind of fairy godmother, producing magical transformations, was acknowledged in 1793, when the pantomime was advertised with the title reversed to read *Mother Shipton Triumphant or Harlequin's Museum*.

This pantomime was notable, first, for the quality and quantity of its music, most of it composed by William Shield, then resident composer at Covent Garden, and later Master of the Queen's Musick. In addition to the specially-written score there were borrowings from composers such as Arne, Arnold, Dibdin, Fisher, Gilliard, Pepuch and Vincent. Some of this was music for dancing – a hornpipe and a burlesque 'pas de russe', for example. But most was for vocal pieces with several of the songs sung by Mother Shipton, the part being played by the actor-singer William Darley.

What attracted the London audiences, though, was not the music, but the impressive succession of clever stage effects, some of them worthy of the best modern illusionists. In an age when we take for granted the devices of trick photography and the fantasy sequences in film and television, we might stand in awe at the elaborate scenery and sophisticated mechanisms already in use on the stage by the end of the eighteenth century. The opening scene of *Harlequin Triumphant*, for example, is a farmyard, complete with animals. In the background is a river on which ducks and swans are swimming. Later there is a flight of ducks, two of which are shot down by sportsmen.

The gist of the story is as follows: Harlequin, disconsolate at the departure of Columbine from the farm, is comforted by Mother Shipton, who promises him protection and gives him a magical sword – as in the 1770 version. The second scene is at the home of Sir Gregory Whimsey, where Columbine is to be married to Squire Foxchase – the latter justifying his name by appearing on stage 'with a real fox and hounds'! In the following scene Harlequin appears from inside a tea urn, performs tricks with candles, and disappears by jumping through a clock, pursued by Clodpole who has charged his blunderbuss with 'tea, sugar, bread and butter, milk etc.' An account of the 1793 production tells us that 'No less than seven of the best pantomime tricks are introduced in this one scene'. Subsequent scenes involve much clowning, including characters pelting each other with vegetables. The pursued Harlequin hides in a dog kennel, which changes into a pigeon house from which real pigeons fly. There is a view of the Tower of London, then the Dockyard, where the ship Loyalty is about to be launched:

The Stage is completely filled with performers. 'God save the King' is sung, three huzzas are heard – the SHIP IS THEN LAUNCHED; after the firing of cannon and every demonstration of joy, a Lieutenant enters and sings the following song ['Hearts of Oak'], which, as it is undoubtedly the most popular ever introduced on a Stage, we present the public with a copy.

[This song had, in fact, been written for the Garrick-Colman production of 1759.]

The most ambitious stage effect of all seems to have been the sudden transformation of the ship into a 'baker's shop' and 'cobler's stall', the latter providing an opportunity for 'truly laughable' slapstick between the 'Cobler, Clodpole, the Pudding-Boy etc.' By means of his magic sword Harlequin sends bottles flying into the air, and later a character called Teague drinks wine from a bottle which then sprouts fireworks by 'a trick of most curious mechanism'

Mother Shipton comes into her own in the Lapland Scene, with its mountains of ice and howling wind, where Harlequin is again in despair, his beloved Columbine having just been recaptured by the Lapland Witch:

Mother Shipton enters in a beautiful CAR drawn by an ELK – the beast, exhausted with fatigue, is seen to die upon the stage – Mother Shipton tells Harlequin to take an enchanted ring from the Witch's finger (who at this time is sunk in repose) and the Spirit of the Witch shall reanimate the body of the ELK – the Elk is seen to rise by degrees, till entirely recovered, and the Witch dies – Harlequin mounts the Car, and taking leave of Mother Shipton rides off to England.

115

Mother Shipton in Christmas pantomime in a carriage drawn by an elk in Lapland.
This illustration appeared in the New Wonderful Magazine (1793)
captioned: 'Mother Shipton's favourite mode of travelling'.
(Brotherton Collection)

The account adds that 'The construction of the ELK in the above scene is reckoned a wonderful piece of workmanship'. So celebrated did this elk become that an engraving of the scene was published in the *New Wonderful Magazine* (1793) showing Mother Shipton in her chariot, wearing a broad-brimmed, pointed hat and with her hooked nose almost meeting her upturned chin – giving us a fair idea of how she was portrayed on stage.

Harlequin is involved in more chasing and disappearing through all kinds of settings, and conjuring tricks and illusions come thick and fast. The scenes are of an incredible variety and complexity: a Cook Shop, a Prison, a Frozen Canal, the Sea, a Crescent in London, a Stationer's shop and the Coal Pit – in which Harlequin is imprisoned. This last scene changes to 'a dark and dreary Cavern, in which Columbine enters with Mother Shipton, supplicating for Harlequin'. Once again the good witch Shipton promises her protection, and produces a happy ending by rescuing Harlequin from his pursuers and persuading Sir Gregory to allow his daughter to marry him.

Mother Shipton now exhibits her amazing powers by transforming the cavern into a scene composed of a magnificent temple, surrounded by actual fountains. There are alcoves studded with diamonds, sapphires, emeralds and topazes, and cupids supporting wreaths of flowers. 'Six trees of astonishing mechanism rise through the stage – they expand to the dimensions of nature, loaded with Oranges of Gold'. The scene closes the pantomime with a dance and chorus – and we can well understand the enthusiasm of the publicist in 1793 who wrote:

After the above description we must candidly declare we can give but a faint idea of the Merits of this Pantomime – the scenery is beautiful in the extreme, the tricks are numerous and excellent . . . the stage is never vacant a moment, and the attention is kept up from the rise to the fall of the curtain – It has been performed 17 nights to crowded houses – and honoured with the presence of Their MAJESTIES, the PRINCE OF WALES, the DUKE OF YORK and CLARENCE, and all the PRINCESSES.

Mother Shipton now had royal approval. Thanks to pantomime, she had changed out of all recognition. Now she was associated with beauty and goodness, and had been deliberately contrasted – in the Lapland Scene – with a wicked witch, whom she had destroyed.

During the nineteenth century, as pantomime developed and its material became more varied, the old 'Commedia dell' Arte' characters were ousted by more popular fairy-tale figures such as Cinderella – and Mother Shipton went with them, being replaced, in a sense, by Mother Goose, who first appeared at Covent Garden on the 26th December, 1806, when Grimaldi was Clown. Yet Mother Shipton had made a contribution both to the tradition of the dame, essentially an older woman played by a man, and also to the tradition of the fairy godmother – played by a woman in *Cinderella*, but with a similar protective role and similar power to effect transformations.

Occasionally we come across a revival of the earlier type of pantomime, such as the production of *Harlequin in Knaresborough* at the Theatre Royal, Harrogate, in 1806; *Harlequin and Mother Shipton* in 1826, when the good witch was accompanied by a mechanical owl and magpie, and a cat played by an actor; and *Mother Shipton* at the Adelphi Theatre in 1855, which involved Harlequin and Columbine. Even in modern times Mother Shipton

117

has not only been presented dramatically, as in the light-hearted show given to local primary schools by the Harrogate Theatre in Education (1988), but she has also continued to play her fairy godmother part in pantomime. In *The Grand Old Duke of York*, written by Norman Robbins in 1981, and still being performed, we are left in no doubt that Mother Shipton is all goodness. She enters 'dressed like a Welsh witch and carries a wooden spoon which is used like a wand'. To the young gypsy-boy Colin, to whom she offers protection, but who recoils at the thought that she is a witch, she retorts:

> Aye, a witch, but one that's good;
> I'd like that clearly understood.

As in the eighteenth-century pantomime, the benevolent Mother Shipton is shown in contrast with a hostile witch, Maleficent, described as 'a bad-tempered fairy'. The essence of the plot is that the two engage in a conflict between good and evil, Mother Shipton supporting the Grand Old Duke of York and Colin (who turns out to be his long-lost son), with Maleficent supporting Baron Snatcher, who attempts to seize York from the Duke.

The Grand Old Duke of York has the customary ingredients of a modern pantomime – audience participation (led mainly by Tommy Tucker), a principal boy (Colin), clowning, chasing and numerous songs. And when chosen a few years ago for their annual pantomime by the Knaresborough Players, it was of great interest to see Mother Shipton making a public appearance in the town of her traditional birthplace, firmly established as the good witch of happy endings.

8

Dickens and the Petrified Army

It came as a surprise to discover that one of the most interesting stages in the evolution of the Mother Shipton mythology was provided – or at least presided over – by none other than Charles Dickens. I had long been familiar with the legend of a king and his army being turned into stone by Mother Shipton – on the boundary between Warwickshire and Oxfordshire. What I had not realised was that the early versions of this story ascribe the petrifaction to a witch who is not named. The first time she is formally identified as Mother Shipton is in an account published by Dickens in 1856. Though this reflects local tradition, there is no doubt that the article which appeared in *Household Words*, under the editorial directorship of Dickens, was the first to publicise Mother Shipton as a witch so powerful she could petrify an army.

The legend concerns what are now called the Rollright Stones, situated a few miles north of Chipping Norton, on the southern side of the A34. They form an impressive group of rugged monoliths, probably dating from the Neolithic period, and consist of the following:

The King Stone, eight feet tall, standing on a hillock.

The King's Men, 76 standing stones in a circle about 100 feet in diameter.

The Whispering Knights, a cluster of four tall stones, like figures huddled together, with another lying flat.

The idea that these stones were really petrified human beings is very ancient. It is similar to traditions about other prehistoric sites, such as the impressive Long Meg and her Daughters in Cumbria – an interesting comparison, because 'Stone Meg' was supposed to have been a sixteenth-century witch, with 77 daughters – all turned to stone for 'soliciting her to an Unlawful love by Enchantment'.

The Whispering Knights
part of the Rollright Stones
traditionally petrified by Mother Shipton

The earliest printed reference to the Rollright legend was made by Camden in 1586, and there seems to have been a much older version in verse. One authority states that these stones are associated with 'one of the richest collections of folklore of any British prehistoric site'. The essence of the story is that a certain king – probably a Viking – was marching north with his knights and his army, intent on conquering the whole of England. As he approached the Cotswold ridgeway between Oxfordshire and Warwickshire he consulted a witch, who spoke to him in the same kind of rhymed prophetic utterance as those associated with Mother Shipton:

> Seven long strides thou shalt take . . .
> If Long Compton thou canst see,
> King of England shalt thou be.

The king strode forward, but as he took the seventh stride a long ridge suddenly rose up before him, preventing him from seeing Long Compton. It is not clear whether the witch caused the ridge to appear by supernatural means, or simply had a sound knowledge of the topography. She did, however, use the occasion to put a curse on the ambitious king and his army:

> As Long Compton thou canst not see,
> King of England shalt thou not be,
> Rise up, stick and stand still, stone,
> For King of England shalt thou be none;
> Thou and thy men hoar stones shall be,
> And I myself an eldern tree.

So the witch, before turning herself into the tree traditionally associated with her craft, namely the elder, turned into stone the king, his knights on horseback, and his army of foot-soldiers. Some of the stones, particularly the Whispering Knights, really do give the impression of primitive human figures, eroded by the centuries.

Other traditions concerning the Rollright Stones (sometimes called the Rollrich Stones) are as follows:

1. The King's Men stones can never be counted, because witches prevent anyone from getting the same number twice. Once a baker is said to have tried to count the stones by placing a loaf on each one, but the loaves were mysteriously moved, and he gave up in despair. Similar stories are told of Stonehenge and other sites. The origin of this idea must be the practical difficulty of locating every stone, some being half-hidden, others resembling each other. I have counted the stones myself, and it took several attempts to confirm the official number.

2. The stones will one day turn into flesh and blood again, and the King will rule over England.

3. The King and the Whispering Knights come alive each midnight (or on certain midnights) and go down to a nearby brook to drink.

4. On Midsummer Eve it was the custom to cut blossom from an elder tree, and when this was done it was observed that the King Stone always moved its head. It was also the custom for young

men and maidens to meet at the Rollright Stones at midsummer and 'make merry with cakes and ale'.

5. Fragments chipped off the Rollright Stones, especially the King Stone, were believed to bring good luck and ward off evil.

6. Removal of any of the monoliths, however, brings bad luck. There are stories of attempts to remove stones for use as bridges or to dam ponds, but the horses pulling the carts, and in one case, two men, were killed, and the stones were always returned.

The Dickens version of the legend appeared anonymously on the 30th August, 1856 in *Household Words*, a weekly family journal he had started in 1850, when he was already firmly established as an author. His declared intention was to provide 'Instruction and Entertainment', in a lively series of articles which he wrote himself or commissioned and edited, the whole forming *Household Words, conducted by Charles Dickens'*. The venture was a great success, sometimes with as many as 40,000 copies sold in a single week.

Though Dickens wrote only a small proportion of the articles himself there is no doubt that he took his editorship very seriously, stamping his personality on *Household Words*, modifying the material, with the result that often we can recognise, in the words of one critic, that it is 'heavy with Dickensian allusions and attitudes'. This is certainly true of the article on Mother Shipton, which is characterised by the kind of ironical humour we associate with Dickens. Yet at the same time, it is presented as a faithful account of material that has been thoroughly researched, 'Nothing can be so damaging to *Household Words*,' wrote Dickens to his sub-editor, W.H.Wills, 'as carelessness about facts'.

The article, simply entitled 'Mother Shipton', is unsigned, but the Office Book of the magazine shows that it was written by a friend of Dickens called Dudley Costello. The latter, having graduated from Sandhurst Military college, had served as an army officer in North America and the West Indies before retiring on half-pay in 1828 to work as a journalist and author. Costello's interest in the supernatural is illustrated by his publication in 1861 of *Holidays with Hobgoblins and Talk of Strange Things*, which includes a reprint of his piece on Mother Shipton.

The Household Words article opens with a passage which shows how familiar Mother Shipton must have been in mid-Victorian England:

There are some names which attain a national celebrity without posterity knowing exactly why or wherefore. That of Mother Shipton is one of the most noted in the traditionary annals of this country. Her fame as a prophetess has extended throughout the land; and her sayings have become, in the remotest corners, literally Household Words.

Costello says that his attention was drawn to Mother Shipton by a recent visit to the Rollright Stones district, where he found that she was the subject of local legend, 'though nothing exists to show that she ever set her foot on the spot'. Before giving an account of the legend he devotes considerable space to an outline of the life of Mother Shipton culled from earlier pamphlets and chapbooks.

This occasionally exhibits the mock-solemn style favoured by Dickens. For example, referring to Toby Shipton, he includes an allusion to a character in *Martin Chuzzlewit*:

He was by profession a builder, though whether he added anything to the glories of the Minster, or acquired a Pecksniffian celebrity for edifices which he never helped to raise, is a point on which no information has been obtained. His fame rests entirely on the fact of his having bestowed his name on the bewitching Ursula; for, with that exception, we hear nothing of him at all . . .
Toby Shipton either crawled through life the most hen-pecked of husbands, or shuffled off his mortal coil after a brief season of conjugal felicity.

Costello's view of the prophecies which brought Mother Shipton to fame is that they were not prophecies at all, but lucky guesses. The following statement of his position, presumably endorsed by Dickens, is worth quoting as an example of the cautious, sceptical approach influenced by nineteenth-century scientific rationalism:

I am ignorant of what period of her life the gift of prophecy descended upon Mother Shipton . . . Her first prophetic essays were probably a few ambiguous words based upon shrewd observation . . . the obscurity in which they were couched leaving the event only doubtful. One lucky hit in matters of prognostication is always better remembered than a hundred failures.

Whether or not Mother Shipton simply hazarded a guess rather than foresaw an event, Costello concedes that she appears to have been a most successful soothsayer, extending her predictions to cover national events. To illustrate this he reproduces material from Lilly's version of 1645, dealing mainly with the visit to the Shipton home in York made in connection with the prophecy about Wolsey. Commenting on the prophecies concerning the fate of each of the three lords who visited her, Costello observes that 'ambiguity of phrase was Mother Shipton's great resource . . . The prediction concerning Lord Darcy was as vague as astrology itself could have framed it'. He rightly points out that Besley was a key figure and probably the means whereby the prophecies had been handed down:

Of all her contemporaneous admirers Mr. Besly seems to have been the most devoted and the most favoured. It was to him the great lords addressed themselves before they ventured to approach Dame Ursula's habitation . . . I look upon Besly as a sort of semi-wizard, who was in the habit of shutting up his shop in the Micklegate earlier than his neighbours in order to go and pass the evenings with Mother Shipton . . . it is no doubt to Besly that we are indebted for the preservation of such of the sayings of the wife of Shipton as are extant.

Costello (or Dickens?) summarises the prophecies of doom and disaster, enlivening them with sneering little asides, ascribing Lilly's explanations to 'Chorus' and interpolating cynical comments such as 'I picture to myself Mr. Besly bursting into tears at this juncture; but Ursula goes on implacably'.

In more serious mood Costello now turns to the legend he has recorded on a recent visit to the Rollright Stones. His enquiries amongst the countryfolk, especially in the nearby villages of Great and Little Rollright, established that whatever the archaelogical reality of the matter the stones were 'ascribed by local tradition to the agency of Mother Shipton'.

He describes the stones in detail, telling us that his own attempt to count them seemed to support the legend of their uncountability.

He found the counting difficult because many of the stones were 'half-hidden by the soil and long, waving grass'. All five of the Whispering Knights were standing, the tallest being nearly eleven feet. He briefly reviews early scholarly accounts, contrasting the theory that Rollright was a memorial to Rollo the Dane with Stukeley's view that it was druidical.

The locals, however, were convinced that this was an army petrified by Mother Shipton. Their story was that an ambitious king, marching north:

halted his little army for the night on the edge of Whichwood Forest, not far from the spot where now stands the little village of Shipton-under-Whichwood. His reason for pausing there is alleged to have been his desire to confer with the wise-woman, who dwelt at Shipton at that time, and who afterwards bequeathed her name to the place.

He then describes the secret meeting between the king and the witch, as observed by the five knights who followed at a distance. In order to obtain her assistance he proposed a certain compact, but the conditions imposed by Mother Shipton must have proved too exacting:

for high words rose beween the two . . . and her harsh voice was heard to threaten the warrior, who came forth in great wrath from the hut, and strode back to his tent.

Costello found that the locals even claimed to know the route the king followed the next day as he led his army northwards – across Lynham Heath, skirting Knollberry Banks and leaving behind 'the old Saxon mart of Ceapen Northtown' until he came to the ridge. Here is Costello's romanticised version of what ensued:

Suddenly, a female figure appeared on the rising summit of the knoll, and, in the clear morning light, the five knights, who watched the motions of their chief, recognised the unearthly lineaments of Ursula Shipton. The events of the previous night came back to their memories, and they whispered among each other. For an instant, the bold adventurer was lost to their view, but presently he re-appeared; and, as he breasted the last ascent, they heard his voice: 'Out of my way, Hag!' he cried –

If Long Compton I may see
Then king of England I shall be!

But another voice – the voice of Ursula Shipton – exclaimed:

Rise up hill! Stand fast, stone!
King of England thou shalt be none!

She waved her arm as she spoke; the earth swelled; and the ambitious chief, the five whispering knights, and the whole of the warrior's mesnie, were at once transformed to stone!

Costello observes that if the king had been able to take six further strides he would have seen Long Compton, but where from the King Stone stands 'nothing is visible but the hill-side'.

He concludes his article with another local legend which says that Mother Shipton had put a curse on anyone attempting to move one of the Rollright Stones. In this version Humphey Boffin, lord of the manor of Little Rollright, shortly before the Civil War, decided to move the King Stone for use in his own courtyard. The countryfolk warned him that disaster would be unleashed, but he took no heed, and attempted to move the stone in a waggon pulled by four strong horses. They could not budge it, and only when he had increased the horse-power to a team of twenty-four was he able to convey the stone to his home. As soon as it was dark:

an indescribable tumult appeared to surround his house,
waxing louder and fiercer as the night drew on; nothing
was heard but groans and shrieks, the clash of weapons and
the direful din of battle, which noises lasted till the
morning, when all again was still.

This supernatural cacophony was repeated on the two following nights, then the terrified Humphrey on the advice of his wife 'agreed to restore the King Stone to the place where Mother Shipton had commanded it to stand'. The task was easy, a single pair of horses finding it light work. But the change of heart did not save Humphrey Boffin from retribution. Soon afterwards Cromwell's troopers ransacked his home. He was drowned in a well while trying to

126

escape, but his virtuous wife was spared to marry the captain of the troop.

Whatever the locals may have believed in 1856 it seems clear that the village of Shipton-under-Wychwood existed long before Mother Shipton, not the other way round. What seems to have happened is that her name became attached to the old legend of the witch, partly because of this coincidence of names, and partly, perhaps, because of the coincidence of a tradition of petrification suggested by the Dropping Well in Knaresborough.

The Rollright Stones have for centuries been the object of the grossest superstition. In 1742, for example, one visitor recorded that he had chipped off bits of stone from the King, the Knights and Soldiers, 'as hundreds have done before me', so he would have powerful talismans to keep the Devil at bay. Prehistoric sites are invariably surrounded by folklore of this kind, and there is nothing surprising in the association of Rollright Stones with Mother Shipton, when we recall that the most famous stone structure of all, Stonehenge, was traditionally said to have been supernaturally built by her magical predecessor, the prophet Merlin.

The importance of Costello's article is that it not only helped to promote the idea that Mother Shipton had the power to petrify, but also disseminated a full account of the supposed witch and her prophecies to a far wider public than ever before. None of the earlier pamphlets and chapbooks could conceivably have reached anything approaching the tens of thousands of copies of this issue of *Household Words*, especially as it was later reprinted separately, not only by Costello, but by the Knaresborough printer and bookseller A.W. Lowe in 1898, and later in long print-runs by William Parr – though neither gave any acknowledgement of the source in these popular reprints.

What is more, even though the article was written as a piece of entertainment rather than serious research, it bore the imprimatur of that most professional and influential of story-tellers, Charles Dickens.

9

The End of the World

Mother Shipton – the witch who foretold the end of the world! This is the way many people continue to think of her, the idea being given a boost from time to time by journalists, letters to the press and the tourist trade. The story of how this nonsense came about, and how it was nurtured, is one of the most interesting aspects of the Shipton mythology.

Prophets have always been assured of attention when they have dramatically revealed some future castastrophe, especially if they have spoken of the end of all things, the coming of doomsday, the winding up of human affairs at the Last Judgement. The inevitability of this *Dies Irae*, the day of wrath, is a familiar theme in Christian scripture and tradition. When linked with the Second Coming and the inauguration of the millennium – Christ's thousand years of perfect reign on earth – it is a powerful idea in the hands of sects and cults preoccupied with prophecy. In spite of the fact that Jesus taught that no man knows either the day or the hour of the end of the age (e.g. Matthew 25:13), there have always been those who feel commissioned to predict that it is just round the corner.

The earliest Mother Shipton material contains no such millenarian preaching – and this, incidentally, argues for a Tudor rather than a Civil War provenance. Though the prophetess is presented as foretelling certain national disasters, in particular the siege of York, the destruction of London and various episodes of bloody warfare, she never apparently foresaw the end of society – only its radical transformation.

Yet it was only a matter of time before Mother Shipton, with her grim prognostications, would be enlisted as a prophetess of terminal doom. It seemed natural enough to the superstitious to expect something of her. Had not famous contemporaries given their version of the date of doomsday? Nostradamus, for example, was believed to have forecast it for '*L'an neuf cens nonante neuf*' (1999), and the notorious London sorcerer Dr. John Dee, writing in about 1598, was supposed to have foreseen a final cataclysm in 1842.

In the eighteenth century John Wesley complained of the false prophets who constantly purported to foretell calamities – and were undeterred by their failure. There was, for example, William Whiston's prophecy that the world would end on the 13th October, 1736, on which date there was widespread panic in London.

Sporadic end-of-the-world predictions have caused alarm throughout history, but there is no doubt that they were at their most fashionable in nineteenth-century Britain and America. Sometimes they were no more than rumours spreading amongst the uneducated, such as the absurd claim that in Leeds a hen had been laying eggs inscribed 'Christ is coming'. The perpetrator of this hoax was Mary Bateman, 'the Leeds witch', hanged and gibbeted for murder by poison in 1809.

Other predictions were published in the guise of serious studies of the Bible, such as the fanatical writings of the eccentric prophetess Joanna Southcott, who died in 1814. As the century advanced, all the successful millenarian sects came into being – British Israelism, the Mormons, the Seventh Day Adventists, the Christadelphians, the Jehovah's Witnesses – and the general climate of opinion favoured interest in eschatology, the doctrine of 'the last things'.

In this respect the printed versions of Mother Shipton's prophecies must have been a disappointment, for they contained no clear forecast of the end of the world. It is not surprising, therefore, that Yorkshire gossip began to compensate for this deficiency. Two interesting examples can be found in local history, both referring to a threatened collapse. As we have noted, in 1704 the overhanging rock of the Dropping Well in Knaresborough, top-heavy with the calcareous deposit responsible for petrifications, broke away from the main rock, leaving a chasm from five to nine feet wide. A smaller slip towards the river occurred again in 1816. In my rare grangerised copy of Hargrove's *History of Knaresborough* there is a note by Dr. Doran referring to this, in which he says that the locals believed that 'when the rock inclines forward a third time, no less a disaster will be on the eve of approaching than the end of the world'. In 1823, around the time this was written, the third slip occurred . . . and then nothing more was heard of this startling prediction.

The second local tradition concerns something far more dramatic. One of the best-known features of Knaresborough is the railway viaduct which spans the River Nidd, close to the Dropping

Well. The building of this massive structure (90 feet high, 338 feet long, with four arches of 56-foot spans) was almost completed when, shortly after noon on the 11th March, 1848, it collapsed into the river with a thunderous roar. No lives were lost, apart from those of thousands of fish killed by the lime in the mortar. The rumour soon went round the town that the disaster had been foretold. The Harrogate historian William Grainge recorded what he had heard in local dialect:

> 'Mother Shipton allus said 'at t' big brig accross t' Nidd
> should tummle doon twice, and stand fer ivver when built
> t' third time'.

Grainge adds that 'this prophecy was never heard of by anyone until after the catastrophe had occurred'. The viaduct was rebuilt in 1851, and shows no sign of threatening a second collapse. But this kind of apocryphal story is typical of the prophecies attributed to Mother Shipton, and they seem to have an almost indestructible quality in the folk memory.

What seems to have happened with this bridge prophecy is that it has become linked with some reminiscence of the earlier one about the Dropping Well, the 'third time' element signalling the end of the world. The version now current – and one quoted several times in the media around the beginning of the new millennium – is that when 'the bridge falls a third time the world will come to an end'. These garbled versions usually add that 'the bridge has fallen twice already'. This is simply not true of any local bridge. High Bridge was repaired and widened in 1773 and 1829, but there is no record of it falling down.

The earliest example I can find of this fable is an item included in the tradition of 'Tellin' t' tale' – patter composed of snippets of history parroted off by local lads from Victorian times onwards, in order to beg a copper or two from visitors. Oral history and printed versions show that they definitely referred to 'the Railway Bridge', meaning the viaduct. But nowadays nobody seems to know which bridge is meant, a common assumption being that it is High Bridge, no doubt because adjacent to this is the World's End – with its inn-sign depicting the final disaster! This name is found elsewhere (including eighteenth-century Harrogate) for an inn at the entrance to a town or village. The Knaresborough inn was known as 'The World's End' at least as early as in the 1820 Directory, so the name cannot possibly have been given by the 1848 disaster and subsequent rumours like the one noted by Grainge.

Charles Hindley
the Brighton bookseller who, in 1862,
published his sensational version of Mother Shipton's prophecies

In 1862, as nothing about the end of the world had appeared in the early Shipton chapbooks, somebody decided to do something about it. This was Charles Hindley, an astute antiquarian bookseller and small-time publisher of Brighton. Judging the moment exactly right, he published a version of the *Life, Prophecies and Death of the Famous Mother Shipton*, which he claimed was 'reprinted verbatim' from material found in the British Museum, namely Head's edition of 1687. This new and ostensibly authoritative edition of Mother Shipton went out from Brighton to an eager public, and was 'to be had of the Booksellers and at all Railway stations'.

But Hindley's publication was nothing more than a confidence trick. Using some of Head's material he skilfully added his own fabricated prophecies, bringing outmoded 'Old Mother Shipton' very much up to date.

In Hindley's topical version she was seen to be more brilliant in her forecasts than had ever been suspected, predicting all kinds of discoveries and inventions, which in 1862 were already the subject of public discussion.

He saved the spectacular end-of-the-world prediction till last – and we must admire the way he cleverly built up the credulity of his readers by first giving them a series of less momentous items, all impressively fulfilled.

Here are some samples of the bogus prophecies which Hindley put into the mouth of Mother Shipton – still, alas, through ignorance or dishonesty being circulated in the twenty-first century and quoted as authentic:

> Carriages without horses shall go,
> And accidents fill the world with woe.

(Railways, by 1862 some thirty years old, were still feared because of terrible railway accidents. Hindley would certainly have had in mind the horrific accident in Clayton Tunnel, near Brighton, which had happened on Sunday, 25th August the previous year. A locomotive had crashed into the rear of a crowded train, driving it fifty yards into the tunnel, resulting in mangled wreckage, shot through with steam and burning coal, in which 23 passengers died horrible deaths and 176 were seriously injured. This led, incidentally, to a much improved signalling system.)

> Around the world thoughts shall fly
> In the twinkling of an eye.

(A clear reference to telegraphy, invented by Morse in 1832, with submarine cables laid from 1851.)

> Water shall yet more wonders do,
> How strange, yet shall be true.

132

(Interpreted as a reference to spas, especially Harrogate, as a Victorian postcard shows.)

> Under water men shall walk
> Shall ride, shall sleep, shall talk.

(Presumably submarines, the first dating from 1801.)

> In the air men shall be seen
> In white, in black, and in green.

(Balloons, pioneered by the Montgolfier brothers from 1783.)

> Iron in the water shall float
> As easy as a wooden boat.

(The first iron-hulled ship was the Great Britain, launched in 1843.)

> A house of glass shall come to pass
> In England, but alas
> War will follow with the work
> In the land of Pagan and Turk.

(This looks back to the opening of the Crystal Palace in 1851 and the outbreak of the Crimean War in 1854.)

> An Ape shall appear in a Leap Year,
> That shall put all woman kind in fear,
> And Adam's make shall be disputed.

(This refers to Darwin's *The Origin of Species* which had appeared in November 1859. Hindley must have been thinking of 1860, which was a Leap Year.)

For good measure Hindley concocted prophecies to fit earlier times, no doubt feeling that Head in his own fabrications had missed one or two good ones. Why not, for example, arrange for Mother Shipton to have predicted Walter Raleigh's return from America with tobacco and potatoes?

Over a wild and stormy sea
Shall a noble sail,
Who to find will not fail,
A new and fair countree,
From whence he shall bring
A herb and a root
That all men shall suit.

Hindley did not have to dig deep for his material – all taken from general knowledge and contemporary journals. In the case of the couplet about railways it is possible he had come across a prediction attributed to 'the Braham Seer' in Scotland, concerning 'carriages without horses', and William Grainge noted the Yorkshire folklore that Mother Shipton had said:

When carriages without horses run
Old England will be quite undone.

It must have occurred to those who read Hindley's counterfeit that all these so-called prophecies referred to things already in the past. The last two lines of his version, however, took the bold and unprecedented step of actually looking into the future. Given prominence by being placed in a separate category of their own, they read:

The world to an end shall come
In eighteen hundred and eighty-one.

These two lines had more impact than all the rest of the false prophecies – indeed, than all the sayings ever attributed to Mother Shipton. Here at least, it seemed, was a prophetess who had plainly foretold the end of the world.

The revelation that doomsday was to occur in 1881 – less than twenty years away – seems to have made Hindley's chapbook a best-seller, and his fabricated lines were copied and pirated everywhere. Typical of the publications spawned by Hindley's is the penny pamphlet *The End of the World and Other Prophecies by Mother Shipton*, which had sold 16,000 copies by the second edition. In Knaresborough itself countless thousands of postcards poured from the press of Parr's, the local printers, to be sent all over the world. They simply gave as 'Mother Shipton's Prophecies' nothing but Hindley's fabricated verses, concluding with the 1881 forecast.

Such was the influence of Hindley's bogus chapbook from its first appearance in 1862 that the following year it was even picked up by Charles Kingsley. He had referred to Mother Shipton as a prophet of doom in his *Westward Ho!* and now he mentioned her in his famous fantasy *The Water Babies*.

Towards the end of the story, when we read of Tom walking backwards on his journey to the Other-end-of-nowhere, we suddenly find Kingsley satirising the current fashion for predicting doomsday with his exuberant run-through of prognosticators, interest in which had just been given new impetus by Hindley:

No sooner had he got out of Peacepool, than there came running to him all the conjurers, fortune-tellers, astrologers, prophesiers, projectors, prestigitators, as many as were in those parts (and there are too many of them everywhere). Old Mother Shipton on her broomstick, with Merlin, Thomas the Rhymer, Gerbertus, Rabanus Maurus, Nostradamus, Zadkiel, Raphael, Moore, Old Nixon, and a good many in black coats and white ties who might have known better, considering in what century they were born, all bawling and screaming at him, 'Look a-head, only look a-head; and we will show you what man never saw before, and right away to the end of the world!'

As Charles Kingsley testified, not everybody was taken in by Hindley's fake prophecies. And when they were printed in the well-respected antiquarian journal *Notes and Queries* in 1872, with an enquiry by a correspondent as to their source and authenticity, Hindley must have felt the deception had gone far enough. In the next edition of *Notes and Queries*, published on the 26th April, 1873, the editor stated that he had received a letter from Mr. Charles Hindley of Brighton in which he had 'made a clean breast of having fabricated the prophecy' quoted in the last issue and taken from his chapbook of 1862.

But the harm had been done – and in any case the average person did not at first have access to the confession made to the limited readership of *Notes and Queries*. As the 1881 doomsday approached there were strange instances of public alarm, encouraged – if not initiated – by the Hindley spoof. In Somerset, for example, there was a widespread belief that Mother Shipton had predicted that Ham Hill would be destroyed by an earthquake and nearby Yeovil visited by a tremendous flood. This was supposed to take place at noon on Good Friday, 1879. In the early morning of that day many fled in terror from the district, but according to one newspaper account:

large numbers of people – many from a distance – flocked to the spot, or as near the spot as they dare venture, to await, half incredulous, and half in terror, the stroke of twelve and the fulfilment of the prophecy. When, however, the appointed hour had passed, they began to look sheepishly into each other's faces, and to move away. At present in mid-Somerset Mother Shipton and her prophecies are somewhat at a discount.

Nevertheless, as 1881 drew near, a similar combination of curiosity and terror appeared in other parts of the country. William Grainge tells us that in addition to earlier traditions, such as the Shipton prediction of the collapse of the viaduct, there was panic in 1880 in the little village of Fewston in the Forest of Knaresborough. Possibly as a result of the construction of the reservoir, there had been a landslip resulting in serious cracks appearing in a dozen of the houses of this village set high above the valley. Immediately some of the villagers recalled that Mother Shipton had prophesied that the world would end when Fewston slid from its ridge into the Washburn Valley.

Another local tradition recorded by Grainge was that Mother Shipton had prophesied the world would end when the climate changed so radically that 'we should not know winter from summer except by the leaves on the trees'. (As we have seen, a similar tradition was collected in Norfolk.) This one dies hard. In spells of exceptionally mild weather in winter I have had phone calls from journalists asking me whether there was any truth in Mother Shipton's prediction that this was a portent of doomsday!

Yet another Yorkshire tradition claims that the 1881 forecast was taken so seriously that the Huddersfield Choral Society arranged a special performance of Haydn's *The Creation* in order to ensure that the world would survive that fateful year. What is more, people in the West Riding of Yorkshire were favoured with a knowledge of the actual day when the world would end. It was to be on the morning of Thursday the 4th March, 1881. There was, indeed, a performance of

The Creation given by the Huddersfield Choral in the evening of that day, this being the last concert before the choir moved from the Armoury to the new Huddersfield Town Hall. The decision to perform this work must have been taken long before, and without any thought of the scare-mongering prediction, but the local press reported that many of the public had rejoiced over the non-fulfilment of Mother Shipton's prophecy for that day, and at the concert were 'expressing their sense of survival by celebrating the world's creation'.

Hindley's 1881 prediction was certainly the subject of much discussion, and in some minds it was linked with another line in his fabrication:

> The world upside down shall be,
> And gold found at the root of a tree.

This seems to refer to the discovery of gold in Australia in 1851. But the idea of the world being turned upside down as an act of judgement by Almighty God goes back to the prophecy of Isaiah: 'Behold, the Lord maketh the earth empty, and maketh it waste, and turneth it upside down, and scattereth abroad the inhabitants thereof'. (Isaiah 24:1) This vision was naturally associated with the end of the world, and along with inn-signs such as 'The World's End' it was once not uncommon to see the sign of 'The World turned upside down'.

If the world was to be inverted on the Day of Judgement it might seem a good idea to be buried upside down. Though this is mentioned by Swift in *Gulliver's Travels* (1726) it has been argued that it was the Hindley fabrication which actually led to at least three known cases of eccentrics arranging to be buried face downwards – one in Sussex and two in Surrey (The idea is ludicrous, of course, since they would still be face downwards even if the earth was inverted!)

Such is the power of superstitious fear that even in modern times there are echoes of Hindley's 'upside down' image. During the Falklands war I was contacted by a York woman, greatly disturbed by the fact that a picture of Mother Shipton had mysteriously turned upside down in its sealed frame. I went to see her and her husband, found no reason to doubt their conviction that this really had happened – and I even had the picture examined by a woodwork expert to see if it was possible to open the frame. It was – with difficulty and determination . . . When I heard that there was a teenage child in the family at the time I felt there might be a rational explanation for this apparently supernatural phenomenon!

Why did Hindley choose 1881 as the year of doomsday? As an antiquarian and collector of literary curiosities he must have realised this figure was a palindrome – reading the same backwards as forwards. It also read the same when turned upside down. Such dates are regarded with awe by the superstitious, but the most obvious explanation for Hindley's choice is that he wanted a date not too far distant from 1862 – or there would have been less interest in it – and also one that produced a rhyme for his jingle (even if 'come' and 'one' are not a true rhyme). Another possibility is that the choice of 1881 was influenced by the fact that Hindley may have known that two comets – well-known harbingers of disaster – were scheduled to appear in that year.

It is just possible that Hindley had come across 1881 as the date worked out by pyramidologists, such as G.P. Smyth, though Smyth's theory was not published until 1877. A curious pamphlet appeared – in the nick of time – in 1880. This was entitled *The End of the World in 1881-2 according to Mother Shipton, the Great Pyramid of Gizeh and other ancient prophecies*. This opens by explaining that Hindley's date was something he had admitted to having fabricated. To show Hindley was not the first to invent prophecies for Mother Shipton, the writer gives an example (probably culled from *Notes and Queries*) relating to the arrest of conspirators said to be plotting the assassination of all the cabinet. One of them, by the name of Monument, was arrested and sent to the Tower. Someone, on hearing this, said to John Taylor, editor of *The Sun*, 'Ah! Ha! Mother Shipton's prophecy, word for word!' He then quoted the lines:

> When the monument doth come to the Tower
> Then shall fall Rebellion's power.

Taylor printed this in his paper, but later had to admit that it had been a hoax. Still, the 1880 publication seriously claimed that the Great Pyramid of Gizeh provided measurements from which the figure of 1881 or 1882 could be calculated!

Typical penny chapbook
from the years leading up to 1881

The people who took Hindley's 1881 prediction most seriously were, naturally enough, those living near Brighton, where the false prophecy had been produced in his North Street bookshop. Once the dreaded year arrived, we are told:

During the year 1881 the most poignant alarm was aroused in the country districts around Brighton, as indeed it was throughout the whole of rural England, by the suggestion that the end of the world that year had been foretold by Mother Shipton . . . Her alleged prophecies had an extraordinary effect on the popular imagination, especially among the poorly educated and more credulous people all over the countryside, many of whom through the course of the year deserted their homes and spent nights praying in the fields, churches and chapels.

Amongst the educated, however, the reaction was always sceptical, and sometimes cynical. On the eve of the dreaded year there appeared a special Christmas edition of a satirical London journal, *The Showman's Panorama*, entitled *The Showman's Shipton*, mercilessly poking fun at Mother Shipton's prophecy that the New Year would be the very last. There is a two-page cartoon headed by the Hindley couplet depicting a crowd of revellers at a jolly New Year party, mostly political figures involved in the Irish question, with the future Edward VII already crowned as King. The theme is that, far from proving a disastrous year, 1881 will be full of fun. There is a rough drawing of Mother Shipton, with black cat and cauldron, and Hindley's fabrication is given in full, prefixed by the note:

A Fortune-Teller in the reign of Henry VIII, Mother Shipton still wields a potent influence. Incalculable are the numbers of feminine minds disturbed by the final couplet in the subjoined 'Prophecies'. These are said to be copied from an old Manuscript in the British Museum. It is not for me to spoil fun or trade. To sceptics I would only say: 'Find and read the original manuscript – if you can!'

Many had, in fact, tried to see the original of Hindley's verse in the British Museum, and the Reading Room had been overwhelmed with enquiries. *The Secular Review* even claimed to have discovered the originator of the hoax in an attendant named George Ball – but no trace of him could be found at the British Museum.

The assertion in *The Showman's Shipton* that it was mostly females who were alarmed by the end-of-the-world prophecy is borne out by an article which appeared in May, 1881 in *The Girls' Own Paper*. This was written by the novelist Isabella Banks, who had been specially commissioned to reassure the many girls who had been writing in about the prophecy 'which has struck terror into the hearts of not a few credulous people by winding up a catalogue of fulfilments with one unfulfilled couplet'. The offending couplet is then quoted – and it is interesting to observe that either the editor or the novelist has seen fit to change a word in order to get a true rhyme:

> The world to an end shall run
> In Eighteen Hundred and Eighty One.

In her article '*Mother Shipton, the Prophetess*', Isabella Banks assured her readers that the prophecy quoted was a fake. But is the original not in the British Museum? 'Nothing of the kind, my dear girls!' She nevertheless accepted that the prophetess existed, and described an oil-painting of her she had once seen in the back parlour of a shop in North London – allegedly belonging to one of Shipton's descendants. The 'Dame Shipton' of the portrait, wearing a ruff, 'was a person of good position, and of middle age' – not at all like the conventional witch. Mrs. Banks also discussed female headgear of the Mother Shipton period, when women wore hoods. According to the prophetess, she claimed, women would one day wear hats, like men. Though there is no mention of Hindley, the conclusion is unequivocal: the so-called prophecy is 'a modern concoction and an imposture got up for sale'.

A most scathing attack on Hindley was made in M.D.Conway's article 'Monsters', published at the very end of 1881 in the December issue of *Harper's Magazine*. Now that the year was safely over, Hindley – who lived until 1893 – could be given the public thrashing he deserved! The Brighton charlatan is attacked as the one who:

conceived the sorry notion of publishing certain prophecies of his own forging. These fictitious utterances were embodied in that kind of runic doggerel which prevails in the Roxborough Ballads ... [and] obtained a wide circulation among the class which is not accustomed to read *Notes and Queries*

As an example of how widely the fabricated verses had been disseminated, he mentions their appearance in *The Globe* newspaper in 1877, where admiration was expressed that they had been published in '1448'. He refers to the printing of Hindley's forgery on a twopenny postcard 'now sold in vast numbers through the length and breadth of the land', and to 'hundreds of newspaper and candy shops in London', where there are posters proclaiming 'Read Mother Shipton's Wonderful Prophecies'. He also describes a 'sensationally decorated sixpenny booklet' which shows Mother Shipton 'careering amidst comets and stars on her broomstick, the familiars accompanying her in the shape of a cat crouching behind her and an owl perched on her broom handle'.

His friends working in the British Museum have told him that, especially after *The Globe* article, they were dealing with as many as fifty enquiries in a single day . . . Conway expresses the hope that Mother Shipton, as in the illustrated booklet, will be blown sky-high:

I fear it will be impossible otherwise to deliver the English masses from this unhappy piece of miseducation . . . The forger of these 'prophecies' may have been unconscious of the full character of his crime . . . What is mere unsupported denial [i.e. by the staff of the British Museum] against the vast numbers of facts built up into the pyramid whose apex Hindley selects to pedestal his lie?

It so happened, as Old Moore had predicted, that 1881 turned out to be a reasonably good year, both for Britain and the world. It might be assumed, then, that once this end-of-the-world prophecy had been proved false, it would surely be forgotten, except as a mere historical curiosity . . . Not a bit of it! By the simple trick of changing the date it was kept going for the benefit of those with a commercial interest in selling the prophecies. The mischievous couplet now read:

> The world then to an end shall come
> In Nineteen Hundred and Ninety One.

There can be little doubt, as Robert Symes stated on television in

1986, that the culprit was the landlord of the Mother Shipton Inn. The earliest case I have found of the revised date appearing in print is in the booklet *The Life and Prophecies of Ursula Southeil*, published in 1910 by J.W.Simpson. His new booklet was the usual summary of Head (oddly enough setting Agatha's seduction in 1472!) followed by a hotch-potch of predictions, including Hindley's fabrication, copied without comment. The writer of the booklet had no scruples in bringing Mother Shipton into the twentieth century by changing a couple of figures, thus falsifying a falsification.

The Simpson booklet was reprinted many times, and soon this revised 1991 doomsday was being copied and circulated all over the world. I have a considerable collection of cards, newspaper cuttings and duplicated sheets, testifying to how widely this 1991 hoax took root. In some cases it was seen as of less importance than the fact that Mother Shipton could be manipulated to foretell every kind of disaster, including the contemporary deterioration of society. A tract issued by an extreme fundamentalist and puritanical sect in the U.S.A., brazenly issued in the manner of Hindley, claimed that Mother Shipton had been inspired by God to write such drivel as:

> For, in those wondrous far-off days
> The women shall adopt a craze
> To dress like men and trousers wear,
> And cut off all their locks of hair,
> They'll ride astride with brazen brow
> As witches do on broomsticks now;
> Then love shall die and marriage cease,
> And nations wane as babes decrease;
> The wives shall fondle cats and dogs,
> And men live much the same as hogs.

The reason this writer made use of Mother Shipton was that she might help to gain converts, terrified into joining the sect in order to escape the wrath to come during the period inaugurated by 1936:

> For then shall mighty wars be planned,
> And fire and sword shall sweep the land;
> But those who live the century through
> In fear and trembling this shall do . . .

For storms shall rage and oceans roar
When Gabriel stands on sea and shore;
And as he blows his wondrous horn,
Old worlds shall die and new be born.

Half-baked inventions though they are, these verses have been widely copied and circulated in the U.S.A., Canada, Australia and now appear on the internet, where one site claims they were smuggled out of the State Library of New South Wales where 'the originals were kept in a locked room'. They include additional infantile jingles, some 'from the outer wrappings of the scrolls'.

The 1991 forecast became so well-known that towards the end of that year I was approached by journalists who were naturally ready to exploit public curiosity concerning Armageddon. I carefully explained how this nonsense had been foisted on Mother Shipton in Victorian times by Hindley, and then updated – but it made little difference. A few hours before 1991 ended Yorkshire Television broadcast an interview with a venerable guide from the Cave who apparently took it all seriously, asserting – I think, with a twinkle in his eye – that Mother Shipton's prophecies had always come true!

It now looks as though the myth-makers have fallen back on the garbled version of the end-of-the-world bridge-fall once peddled by the lads earning coppers. As I have argued, this is surely nothing more than the saying about a third rockfall, transferred to the viaduct when it collapsed in 1848 – a conflation and confusion, rather than a fabrication. It has the advantage, of course, of not being attached to any predicted date – and the appearance of a crack in the masonry could sharpen interest dramatically at any time.

Anyone who doubts this should remember the fuss at the beginning of July 1999 when the media started gossiping about this month being destined for the coming of the 'King of Terror' according to Nostradamus.

Channel 4's Big Breakfast Show decided to interview Martin Weeks, Chief Engineer of Harrogate Borough Council, to assure viewers that Knaresborough's bridge (in this case, High Bridge rather than the viaduct) was perfectly sound. About six hours after his assurance that it was, a freak storm of torrential rain descended on Knaresborough, lifting the tarmac on the bridge and causing it to be closed to traffic. Instant hysterical speculation! More fuss in the press and on television. Was this a sign of the end of the world?

The notion that Mother Shipton was the recipient of apocalyptic visions will be hard to eradicate. One prediction we can make with absolute confidence. Although she did *not* foretell the end of the world, there will always be people eager to say and believe that she did. You can always make a propaganda if you have the proper geese.

Mother Shipton riding through the night sky
(From the cover of a typical penny Prophetic Almanac)

10

The Resilience of Mother Shipton

The commercial exploitation of Mother Shipton has been going on ever since her appearance in the first known pamphlet in 1641. Since that date, I estimate that there have been perhaps a hundred different printed editions of assorted prophecies, many of them going through untold reprints.

These have given birth to versions on postcards, and on slips in Christmas crackers, with the name of the prophetess gracing all kinds of fortune-telling chapbooks. So the quaint corpus of Shipton material has grown like an ever-rolling snowball, most recently being proliferated through the internet.

A marked increase in exploitation came, first, after the Great Fire of 1666, when Richard Head cashed in on public interest in the alleged Shipton prophecy, and, secondly, in late Victorian times, when Charles Hindley managed to pass off as genuine, a series of spectacular predictions of his own devising.

There have been fluctuations in her popularity, but Mother Shipton has proved to be remarkably resilient. In 1822 Edward Baines noted that her prophecies were 'falling into disrepute and neglect' and thought that with the advance of education it would only be a matter of time before they disappeared altogether. Yet, in the twenty-first century Mother Shipton's prophecies are still available, with Hindley's spurious version still being sold and quoted as Gospel truth.

Nor has it been just the prophecies. The magical yet benign version of Mother Shipton presented in many a pantomime and chapbook made her an ideal name to promote the sale of a variety of household and pharmaceutical products. We have, for example, a Victorian soap manufacturer (Goodwin's of Manchester), advertising three-penny bars of 'Mother Shipton's Soap', perhaps mindful of the popularity of the prophetess with East Anglian washerwomen! The soap was so good that they could advertise washdays with 'No Boiling'. The adverts included an attractive coloured picture of the smiling prophetess and the jingle:

Back-weary Woman Go to Bed:
Let Mother Shipton wash instead!

The association of wise-women with the gathering of herbs and the preparation of secret but efficacious remedies made Mother Shipton a powerful name to endorse a medicine or ointment. In 1891 the public were offered:

The Best Healer in the World
MOTHER SHIPTON'S SALVE
Cures all kinds of Sores, Bad Legs, Boils
Carbuncles, Bad Breasts etc. when every
other remedy has failed.

Testimonials to the efficacy of this ointment could be obtained 'on application to the Sole Proprietor', W. Forster of Knaresborough, but it was sold (in boxes at 7½d, 1/1½d and 2/6d) in many other places 'by all respectable Patent Medicine Vendors'. It was still being sold in Knaresborough in 1907, now with V. Thompson as the sole Proprietor, who claimed it to be 'A positive cure for Eczema and All Skin and Eruptive Diseases', and printed testimonials in his adverts.

This panacea does not appear to have been sold by the Lawrence family at the famous Oldest Chemist's Shop in England, in Knaresborough Market Place, no doubt because they were selling several remedies of their own manufacture, especially their Old English Lavender Water, made on the premises to a traditional recipe. Another chemist, Charles Southwell, was selling 'The Knaresborough Bouquet', a perfume admired by Lillie Langtry and Ellen Terry. By 1907 his successor, S. Day, was selling it as 'The Nidd Valley Bouquet', and a few years later, not to be outdone, J.W. Simpson was offering to his Mother Shipton visitors bottles of 'Dropping Well Lavender Water', at prices ranging from 9d to 5/6d.

Novelties of this kind, as well as the sale of petrified objects and booklets about the Dropping Well and Mother Shipton, were of less financial importance than the simple influx of visitors . . . Knaresborough's economy has been based in turn on the Castle and its garrison, on a thriving market once famous for liquorice, cherries and especially corn, on the spa trade, on linen manufacture, and in recent years on small businesses and light industry, with a rapid expansion in housing for commuters and the retired. But ever since the early sixteenth century a small but important part of Knaresborough's economy has been tourism.

From at least Tudor times one of Knaresborough's principal attractions has been the unique Dropping Well. As previous chapters have shown, it was the well itself which people came to see in the earlier centuries. Mother Shipton, if she was mentioned at all, was a mere accessory, mentioned in passing. It is significant that in the advertisements publicising the Dropping Well at the end of the nineteenth century, when Frederick Comer was the lessee, there is not even a mention of Mother Shipton.

As we have seen, all this changed when J.W.Simpson, a former proprietor of the Crown in High Street, took over from the Comer family in 1909. In the adverts for that year, though he retained the wording used by his predecessors, urging visitors not to fail to see 'the far-famed Dropping Well', he added 'and Mother Shipton's Cave'. At the bottom of the advert he is styled 'J.W.Simpson, Proprietor' – though in the catalogue of the Slingsby estate, sold by public auction in 1916, it is stated that Simpson, landlord of the Mother Shipton Inn, had held this and the Dropping Well estate 'on lease for 21 years from 1st February, 1910 at an annual rent of £110'. At any rate, in 1916 he became the owner of Lots 30 and 31, this profitable segment of Slingsby land, and it remained in his family until 1986.

The Mother Shipton industry, as distinct from the Dropping Well trade, came into its own in the Simpson era. Not content to be a mere landlord with a natural curiosity in his grounds, he began to promote the prophetess, and he could not have wished for a better start than the royal visit he presided over in July, 1910, reported in the press as follows:

. . . accompanied by Her Imperial Highness, the Grand Duchess George of Russia, and the Princesses Ninon and Ksanea, the Princess Victoria covered the short distance from Harrogate to Knaresborough by motor car, and on arrival at High Bridge the party alighted and made their way on foot through the picturesque Long Walk to the famous Dropping Well, so closely associated with the name of the prophetess, Mother Shipton.

Here the various objects of interest were explained by the proprietor,

Mr. Simpson, and the numerous articles and rare birds and animals suspended from the rock in process of petrifactiion were a source of wonderment to the party, and especially to the younger Princesses. Curiosity was also evinced in the Wishing Well, which was entered and afforded some amusement. The cave reputed to have been the habitation of Mother Shipton was inspected, after which a considerable time was spent in the museum attached to the hotel, where Princess Victoria made purchases of tokens worked from stone at the well.

This account rightly stressed the picturesque nature of the Long Walk, which offers such delightful views of the old town rising above the river, crowned by the ruined Castle. Then there is the great weir which, from 1764, supplied the town with water and helped to power Walton's mill on the opposite bank, supplier of linen to all the royal household. It was this sylvan parkland, as much as the well and cave, which appealed to visitor and resident alike. At that time it was possible to enter it by crossing the Nidd on the 'Penny Ferry' operated for many years, man and boy, by George Smith from the end of Sturdy's boat landing, near the moored house-boat café, the Marigold. The townsfolk, no less than royalty, had access to the Long Walk, either from the main entrance at High Bridge, or from behind the inn, near Low Bridge. Within living memory it was possible for local people to hold a key for five shillings a year, enabling them to enter by a small gate next to the main High Bridge entrance. To pass through the estate the general public paid a penny.

Cooperation between the Dropping Well estate and the town was at its height during Knaresborough's famous Water Carnivals. The flat part by the river, now used as a car-park, formed a kind of stage on which sets were sometimes built – a large fairy palace, for example. In the 1899 Water Carnival the 'electric searchlight' picked out the figure of Mother Shipton leading a procession of illuminated boats down the river, and sometimes there was the spectacular backcloth of the viaduct, transformed by Brock's fireworks into a simulation of Niagara Falls.

As the twentieth century unfolded, the image of Mother Shipton as a magical but attractive personality was presented to the public, mainly through advertising and new editions of the Simpson booklet. In Harrogate there was an amused tolerance of her, reflected in 1926 in the publication of a satirical song by Cumberland Clark in which he complained that Mother Shipton had failed to forecast such things as half the population on the dole, the fox-trot craze, women smoking and voting, Oxford bags, prohibition and the cinema. In 1936 there appeared a petrol advert playing on the popularity of the Dropping Well. It showed the prophetess rising from her hospital bed with the caption: 'Mother Shipton's well – but SHELL'S better!' A glance through the guide books produced by the Knaresborough Urban District Council, and after 1976 by the Harrogate Borough Council, shows that the tourist trade had by this time accepted without question that the cave itself, and not merely Knaresborough, was Mother Shipton's birthplace.

Mrs. Shirley MacLean, a great-niece of J.W. Simpson, was responsible for updating and extending publicity. The press was, of course, quick to pick up any suggestion of supernatural phenomena connected with the cave. In 1975, when Mrs. MacLean had spent £10,000 on a new floodlighting scheme, and had installed a large effigy of Mother Shipton in the cave, there were reports of inexplicable damage, including the Geller-like bending of strong metal bars, problems for press photographers, and an accident to a reporter, who slipped awkwardly and ended up in hospital. 'Mother Shipton casts a spell on her old haunts' is typical of the headlines that appeared, providing excellent free publicity.

There were still supernatural overtones. Mrs. Maclean's souvenir booklet included material sent to her by spiritualist mediums. 'We are told that in Australia', she wrote, 'there is a lady who feels herself to be an incarnation of Mother Shipton, and who has actually published prophecies which she believes are directly from the Prophetess'. Not to be confused with this were leg-pulling appropriations in the tradition of Head and Hindley. In 1975, when I first stood for election to Knaresborough Town Council, I made up a comic Shipton prophecy for my canvassing leaflet which ended:

Who shall win? I'll not foretell it –
But spare a vote for Arnold Kellett!

In 1992 the supernatural element was revived by the Knaresborough Chamber of Trade with a new visitors guide which included a page of horoscopes provided by 'Stella Shipton' who, according to the caption, was 'reputed to be the great, great, great niece of Mother Shipton'. (It would have required ancestors of antediluvian longevity to take this line back to Tudor times!) On a higher level poets have claimed to have been inspired by the spirit of the prophetess. In 1998, for example, a Rochdale man, Steve Anderson, published his poems about Mother Shipton and the town under the title *Alchemy of Passion*, now advertised on the internet:

> Fulfilling that legendary puzzle
> Still out there in cyberspace
> Nothing will stop her:
> Millennium Witch,
> Surfing about on her broomstick.

In the second half of the twentieth century pilgrimages to the shrine of Mother Shipton remained popular. Mrs. MacLean claimed that in 1976, a year with a long hot summer, the total number passing through the Dropping Well Estate was 240,000. The weather has naturally been a major factor in visitor numbers, but the average has been quoted as not much below 100,000 and the figure for 1997 was given to the Harrogate Borough Council publicity officer as 156,000. In August 1996 the millionth visitor was recorded and the press reported the delight of the family who had recently moved to Harrogate, when they were presented with a certificate, a lavish meal and a 'petrified cuddly toy'.

Such figures show that the business had survived a major, much-publicised set-back ten years earlier. In June 1986 Mrs. MacLean sold the 12-acre Dropping Well Estate to a company called Maximum Entertainment Limited. What hit the headlines was that one of the new owners was the internationally-famous stage and television illusionist, Paul Daniels. The major shareholder and managing director was Frank McBratney, who for the past six years had been general manager of Wookey Hole Caves in Somerset.

The new management immediately speeded up the earlier shift in emphasis from the petrifying well to the prophetess. Henceforth the business was not to be known as 'The Dropping Well Estate', but 'Mother Shipton's Cave, Ltd.' Very soon there was a redesigned entrance, the planting of 300 trees and other improvements. Then in February 1987 the company submitted a planning application for a visitors centre, restaurant, toilet block and bandstand on the riverside – in the most prominent part of the famous view from Knaresborough Castle.

This application sparked off lively controversy and was rejected the following month by the Harrogate Borough Council, mainly because of its 'intrusion into the natural setting on the River Nidd to the detriment of the character and amenities of the area'. The company approached the Council to see if some modified plan might be acceptable and arranged for Paul Daniels to confront enquirers and critics. About 200 crowded into the Mother Shipton Gift Shop to meet him. Many were supporters, and the atmosphere was amicable – though the local press could not resist the headline:

Daniels in the lions' Den
Residents vent fury on TV star over Mother Shipton plans.

Modified plans for the new visitors centre, though strongly supported by the Knaresborough Chamber of Trade, were opposed by Knaresborough Town Council, Knaresborough Civic Society, the Council for the Protection of Rural England, the Nidd Action Group and a petition signed by 2,539 objectors. Even the then Poet Laureate, Ted Hughes, sent in a written protest. In November 1988, after Paul Daniels had withdrawn from the company, an enquiry was opened in Harrogate by the Department of the Environment. The case for allowing modern development was compelling on economic grounds, but the appeal was finally rejected by the Inspector (Judy Crane) on environmental grounds, with the York Georgian Society, English Heritage and others (including myself) arguing that this beautiful stretch of riverside woodland was a remarkable survival from the spa period – as the term 'The Long Walk' implies.

Though a set-back for the company, tourists continued to come in encouraging numbers. In 1992 the manager, now Robert McBratney, deftly turned to his advantage a strange piece of publicity provided by a visitor from Manchester. This man had complained to Knaresborough Town Council of 'cruelty to teddy bears', saying that he had seen the look of distress on the faces of children at the Dropping Well when they saw the bears being strung up under the dripping water to be turned into petrifactions. 'How many cuddled their teddies that night,' he asked, 'in fear of the men who take them to be turned to stone?' This complaint – apparently made in all seriousness – was enthusiastically taken up by the media, thus providing Mother Shipton's Cave Ltd. with undreamed-of publicity spiced with humour. 'We vigorously refute these claims,' stated the tongue-in-cheek managing director, 'and deny any allegations that we have ill-treated teddy bears'.

Mother Shipton enlists in World War II
A wartime poster calling on the people of Knaresborough to
help Mother Shipton 'sweep away the Nazis' by
supporting a National Savings Warship Week.

Over the years there have been various kinds of publicity – such as special events at Halloween, Psychic Fairs, The End of the World Hotline, and the celebration of 'Mother Shipton's 500th Birthday'. This should have taken place in the July of 1988 (that is, for those who seriously accept the Conyers date of July, 1488), but there had been so little support that nothing official had materialised. Then

Mrs. Joyce Hawley stepped in, set up a committee and arranged a series of crowd-pulling events to raise money for charity. The celebration took place on the 17th September, 1988, reported in the *Knaresborough Post* under the headline: 'Happy Birthday, Mother!'

Led by the Town Crier, Mother Shipton in person, played by Mrs. Hawley, rode on horseback from the Mother Shipton Inn, up through the town and down to the Cave. There was even a 'Mother Shipton's Birthday Cake' made by one of the town's bakeries.

Mother Shipton being interviewed by the author
during the Millenium Pageant, Knaresborough Castle

This was not the first time Mother Shipton had been resurrected. She regularly appeared in the Water Carnival in late Victorian and Edwardian times – and in revivals in the 1950s. I have even resurrected her myself in the historical pageants I wrote and presented in 1972 and 2000, the latter being the colourful Knaresborough Millennium Pageant. On each occasion I stood on the battlements of Knaresborough Castle calling forth a succession of remarkable characters from Knaresborough's rich heritage. It was a great pleasure, both in 1972 and 2000, to interview Eileen Cosgrove, who convincingly played Mother Shipton as a plain-spoken, independent-minded woman with a strong local accent, and a touch of charisma:

Oh, aye . . . Cardinal Wolsey thowt we'd mek such a fuss aboot 'im bein' oor Archbishop — But Ah telled ivverybody . . . Ah says, 'Wolsey may *see* York, but 'e'll nivver reach t' city . . . An' 'e stood theeare on t' top o' Cawood Castle . . . 'When Ah get ti York,' 'e says, 'Ah'll 'ave yon woman (meanin' *me!*) *burnt* as a *witch!* Aye. Those were 'is very words, sir! But, d'yer knaw? T' minute 'e said this, an officer clapped an 'and on 'is showlder — an' arrested 'im on a charge of 'igh treason! So Ah wor reight, yer see! Wolsey *saw* York, but 'e nivver got theeare!

That is something like the woman I imagine to have been at the core of the Mother Shipton story. And, at the beginning of a new millennium, it was good to bring her to life in this way. Not that she needed much help. Mother Shipton seems to have a life of her own. Her popularity may vary, but she comes back again and again. Like the nebulous Nostradamus, both she and her prophecies are still around. She survives because she is a paradox . . . an infallible oracle, yet derided as a fake; a diabolical witch, yet a fairy godmother benefactress; a hideous crone, yet an appealing wise-woman; a figure devoid of historical substance, yet, for many, larger than life. People can make of her what they will, this incomparable oddity from the past – but she will survive as the perennial female prophet, a peg on which to hang many a fanciful claim, unique in the folklore of the world.

As the old pantomime song had it:

There's none like Mother Shipton!

Those who have carefully read through this book will have seen the wide variation in attitudes to her. At one extreme we have the starry-eyed veneration of those who not only believe she was a real person, but who claim she is still speaking to us through her printed oracles or even mystical contact. At the other extreme are those who have dismissed her with contempt as an old fraud. 'That such a person lived may be true,' conceded William Camidge of York, a fellow of the Royal Historical Society, 'and that she made a cosy living by fortune-telling is equally likely, but that she uttered any prophecies is a matter of the greatest improbability'. William Grainge, writing in the *Palatine Notebook* in 1881, had gone even further. Mother Shipton, he asserted, was 'a unique creation of credulity and trickery. A name, and nothing more'. This is the position of many an academic today. Whilst not denying the possibility of precognition and the prediction of future events, many regard Mother Shipton as an invention, like one of the witches in the fairy tales collected by the Grimm brothers.

To round off with a summary of my own view, based on the years of research and reflection which underpin this book, I would like you to accompany me on a visit to the Dropping Well. In 2001 this was taken over by a new owner, Adrian Sayers, but it is essentially as it has been for the past 500 years . . .

If we can choose a quiet time and have the place to ourselves, so much the better . . . What an atmosphere is here! The mysterious-looking bulge of gleaming, tawny rock, with its attractive striations and silver curtain of ever-tinkling water – an unfailing 700 gallons of it every hour . . . The unusual combination of sight and sound – and smell. There is the dank air of the river, the scent of the surrounding mature woodland, with its tang of wild garlic, the whole area since 1989 included by English Heritage in the Register of Parks of Special Historical Interest.

Now look up at the objects hanging under the trickling water to be petrified – gloves, hats, teddy bears . . . the ones there the longest being more difficult to recognise under their encrustation of stone . . .

Well, I think that Mother Shipton is like one of these objects hung up to petrify. Over the years she has been grotesquely deformed by all the layers of legendary accretion. But underneath there is a real Yorkshirewoman, a carpenter's wife, something of a character, speaking out in the days when women were expected to keep quiet, dubbed 'the Sibyl of York' because of her fondness for turning out prophetic rhymed couplets.

And, on the whole, I think it fortunate that, throughout all her years of soothsaying, she was apparently spared a vision of what succeeding generations would do to her!

Bibliography

(A small selection of books and journals consulted. No attempt
has been made to give a full list of all the versions of the prophecies.)

The Prophesie of Mother Shipton in the Raigne of King Henry the Eighth,
Printed for Richard Lownds, London, 1641.

*A True Coppy of Mother Shipton's last Prophesies as they were taken from
one Joan Waller*, London, 1641.

Foure Severall Strange Prophesies, Printed for R.Harper, London, 1642.

Nuncius Propheticus, London, 1642.

Ancient and Moderne Prophesies by William Lilly, London, 1645.

*Mother Shipton's Prophecies, with three and XX more, all most terrible and
wonderful* Printed by T.P. for F.Coles, London, 1662.

The Life and Death of Mother Shipton by Richard Head, London, 1667,
(editions also in 1684, 1687 and later reprints).

Mother Shipton's Christmas Carrols, Printed by and for P.Lillicrap,
London, 1668.

*The Life of Mother Shipton: A New Comedy, as it was Acted Nineteen dayes
together with Great Applause* by T. Thompson, London, (?1668).

The Strange and Wonderful History of Mother Shipton, Printed for W.H.
and sold by J.Conyers, London, 1686.

Eboracum by F.Drake, York, 1736.

The renowned Mother Shipton's Most surprizing Yorkshire Prophecies,
London, 1740.

The History of the Castle, Town and Forest of Knaresborough, by
E.Hargrove, York, 1775.

A Correct Account of Harlequin's Museum or Mother Shipton Triumphant,
London, 1793.

The New Wonderful Magazine Vol.II, p.225, London, 1793.

Wonders, Past Present and to Come, Reprinted for S.Baker, London, 1797.

Mother Shipton's Legacy or a favourite Fortune Book, York, 1797.

The Spas of England by A.B.Granville, Vol.I, London, 1841.

Household Words ed. Charles Dickens, London, Vol.XIV, 1856.

The Life, Prophesies and Death of the Famous Mother Shipton
(spurious edition by Charles Hindley), Brighton, 1862.

Notes and Queries, 4th Series, Vol. XI, p.355, London, 1873.

On an Inscribed Stone at Orchard Wyndham by W.George, Bristol, 1879.

The Palatine Notebook Vol.I, article by W.Grainge, Manchester, 1881.

Mother Shipton Investigated, by W.H.Harrison, London, 1881.

Holroyd's Ballads ed. G.B.Forshaw, London, 1892.

Mother Shipton: The Yorkshire Sibyl by William Camidge, York, 1898.

The Itinerary of John Leland ed. L.T.Smith, London, 1907.

A Book about Yorkshire by J.S.Fletcher, London, 1908.

The Diary of Samuel Pepys ed. H.B.Wheatley, London, 1928.

Witch Hunting and Witch Trials by C.L'Estrange Ewen, London, 1929.

Motif Index of Folk Literature ed. Stith Thompson, Copenhagen, 1952.

The Life and Death of Cardinal Wolsey ed. R.S.Sylvester, Oxford, 1959.

A History of Yorkshire and the City of York ed. P.M.Tillot, London, 1961.

English Historical Review, article by H.Rusche, 'Prophecies and Propaganda', lxxxiv, London, 1969.

Religion and the Decline of Magic by Keith Thomas, London, 1971.

A Dictionary of British Folk Tales ed. K.M.Briggs, 1971.

The Folklore of East Anglia by E.Porter, London, 1974.

The Folklore of Somerset by K.Palmer, London, 1976.

Mother Shipton's Prophecies Reprint by George Mann, (with introduction from *Old Yorkshire*, ed. W.Smith, 1883), Maidstone, 1973.

Historic Knaresborough by Arnold Kellett, Otley,1991.

The New National Dictionary of Biography, article by Arnold Kellett, Oxford, 2004.

About the Author

Dr. Arnold Kellett has for many years been a popular speaker and writer, particularly concerning the Mother Shipton town of Knaresborough, where he taught at King James's School from 1956 to 1983. He has twice served as Mayor of Knaresborough, and in 2001 was made a Freeman of this historic North Yorkshire town.

An authority on dialect as well as local history, he is the author of a score of books, including *The Yorkshire Dictionary of Dialect, Tradition and Folklore*. The Yorkshire Society has awarded him the prestigious Yorkshire History Prize for his research establishing that Knaresborough was the scene of the first known Royal Maundy, given by King John in 1210, and also the Bramley History Prize for his work on Mother Shipton. Most recently he has been invited to write the article on Mother Shipton for the *New National Dictionary of Biography*.